CONVERSATIONS ON THREE CONTINENTS

M. H. Velshi

CONTENTS

PREFACE

INTRODUCTION

I. MIGRATIONS: OUT OF INDIA AND AFRICA
II. CANADA
III. THE FIRST TRIP
IV. TRAVELS WITH ABID
V. RETURN TO MUMBAI
VI. TEACHING AND EXPLORING
VII. RETURNING HOME

PREFACE

I am often asked the question, usually by other immigrants," Where are you from? India?"

Unable to come up with a simple and concise answer, my mind responds with a flood of memories.

Sometimes I remember the city I was born in, full of gardens, parks, wide boulevards and large trees, especially my favourites, the massive Eucalypti with their peeling bark and sharp scent.

Sometimes I recall walking to school in Nairobi alongside a line of green British Leyland trucks filled with Tommies laughing and waving at us, remember the fear of living through the Mau Mau war that followed and finally the euphoria of independence. The great hopes of building a new country turned into bitter disillusionment. Paradise lost but never forgotten.

Often I remember arriving in Toronto on a snowy, cold day in December 1974. I have now spent the better part of my life in Toronto, a city of harsh winters that has turned, from a provincial place, into a city of marvelous diversity.

Finally my great curiosity about the land of my ancestors led me to India. Between 1992 and 2008 I made four trips during which I explored parts of the subcontinent, searched for relatives, worked as a business consultant and volunteered in an inner city school in Mumbai, alongside my wife, Najma, a teacher.

After my last trip I decided to write a book about my experiences of India but memories and reflections from the past wound their way through my narrative turning it into a travel memoir; Conversations on Three Continents, an attempt to answer the frequently asked question of where I am from with greater clarity.

Some of the episodes in this story such as my father's visit to Mumbai are as close as I can recollect from my conversations with him and with additional research I have endeavoured to present facts as far as that is possible.

I want to thank my wife Najma and our dear friend Linda Stanyer, whose encouragement and guidance have helped me through three years work of writing this memoir. I also want to thank my editors Kathryn Dean and Aimee Madill, without whose help this work may not have got published and my daughter Sameena who often challenged me with the words, "You always tell me you can do anything you put your mind to, don't you?"

INTRODUCTION

The Ismailis: A brief history
I belong to a people who've never had a homeland.

Spread over thirty countries, the Shia Ismailis speak a multitude of languages, from English to Tajik, and trace their roots back to the Middle East, Central Asia, and the Indian subcontinent.

The Muslim world or the Ummah, is made up of two main branches, the Sunni and the Shia. Although both groups subscribe to the main tenets of Islam, the Sunnis believe that Mohammed was the last prophet. The Shias believe that his son-in-law, Ali and his successors had the authority to lead them after the Prophet's death. This difference has led to a deep division. Over time the Shia split into several sects, the Ismailis being one of them.

The forging of the Ismaili identity has occurred against a backdrop of migrations, conversions, expulsions and genocidal attacks. The early migration path, starting from Arabia, included Syria, Iraq, Morocco, Tunisia, Egypt, Persia, Central Asia, China, the subcontinent of India and finally Africa, Europe and North America.

In the early tenth century, the Ismaili Imams began to establish the Fatimid Empire in North Africa. At the peak of their power, they founded the city of Cairo and ruled Egypt for over two centuries. During the twelfth century, Christian crusaders as well as the Sunni armies of Saladin began attacking the Ismailis. The Shia Fatimid Empire was replaced by a Sunni caliphate in Egypt and the Ismaili population became concentrated in Syria and Persia.

In 1256 Hulagu Khan, grandson of Genghis Khan, led a devastating attack on an Ismaili fort in Alamut,

Persia, killing most of the men, selling off the women and children into slavery, and destroying libraries of precious religious texts. The survivors and their descendants went into hiding for many decades.

Starting in the late fourteenth century, the Ismaili Imams of Persia sent Pirs to India to spread the Ismaili faith. Most of those converted came from the lower Hindu castes, living in the northwestern part of India. My forefathers, probably peasant farmers from Gujarat, converted to Ismailism but were forced to practice their new religion as Guptis (hidden followers) to avoid persecution by Hindus and the Muslim Sunni majority. The Imam of the nineteenth century, Aga Khan I, became the first Ismaili leader to move to India from Persia.

Around the turn of the last century, Ismailis from India began migrating to Africa, primarily to Kenya, Uganda, Tanganyika and Zanzibar. These settlers became traders, farmers, clerks, and railway workers who, along with other Indians, helped the British in colonizing East Africa. The hinterland had swathes of fertile lands ideal for planting tea, coffee and cotton, virgin forests for lumbering and herds of game for ivory, skins and hunting.

In the last century, Sir Sultan Mohammed Shah, Aga Khan III, started programs to transform the Ismaili community. He promoted the building of schools, housing colonies, and hospitals, particularly in India, Pakistan, and East Africa, and encouraged greater emphasis on education and women's rights. He became the first Imam to move to the West. Prince Karim Shah, Aga Khan IV, the present Imam, born in Switzerland, and educated at Harvard, has carried on with his grandfather's vision on a far larger scale.

The political storms of the twentieth century, starting with the Partition of India and Pakistan, disrupted the plans and the lives of those Ismailis living in India. During the unrest the majority was forced to flee into the predominantly Sunni Muslim Pakistan. Some, caught up in the bloody division, were killed, but the majority survived and started new lives in Pakistan, albeit as a minority.

Soon after Indian independence, African countries also began to demand their freedom and following widespread unrest in the Fifties, the British started to withdraw from the continent. The majority of the Ismailis living in Africa took up the new citizenship of their adopted country whilst a few retained British citizenship and moved to England.

Those that stayed behind, under the direction of the Imam, eliminated racial segregation in its community-built schools and hospitals and began to invest heavily in the African economy. But the great hope of a stable and multicultural society was to be dashed within a decade as Tanzania adopted socialism, nationalizing all private property; the Ugandan dictator Idi Amin expelled all Asians from the country, confiscating their assets and Kenya sank into corruption.

For the Ismailis, Africa's political strife resulted in yet another set of migrations, this time to the West. Thousands from Uganda and the neighbouring countries, often stripped of their assets, moved to Canada, Britain, and the U.S. The majority of Ismailis, however, still live in developing countries like Pakistan, Afghanistan, and Tajikistan and continue to face persecution and upheavals.

Through the centuries Ismailis have developed an ability to settle in new countries and yet maintain a powerful sense of identity, traditions and faith. Great emphasis is still placed on education, particularly for women, and on volunteerism

Mine is the story of a family's seventy-year journey of migration across three continents to escape political convulsions, prejudice and poverty. Immigration, as I have come to learn, is not just about moving from one country to another. It's much more about moving from one culture to another, a journey that never quite ends.

I. MIGRATIONS: OUT OF INDIA AND AFRICA

"Poverty and pride are like the devoted blood brothers until one, always and inevitably, kills the other."

Shantaram by Gregory Roberts.

1. Mumbai, 1934.

They took a long walk during the last afternoon of his stay in Mumbai.

The hot day suddenly felt cooler when they reached Marine Drive and they paused to inhale the salty evening breeze that rushed in from the blue Arabian Sea to cleanse and refresh the city.

Anil glanced sideways at Bai, his eldest sister, who was more of a mother to him than a sibling. She had raised him from birth until she was married off to Hussein and left their tiny Gujarati village for Mumbai. Seven years old, he had cried for weeks and Ma spent what time she could spare to console him.

Thankfully, this arranged marriage had turned into a loving relationship. Over the seven years since her wedding, Bai had changed from a lanky, serious girl who had taught him his numbers and alphabet to a fashionably dressed woman with a fulsome figure, the mother of two boys and a girl. Anil was used to seeing the women in the village wear plain cotton saris but Bai wore silk, often blue, and large gold bangles, especially when they went to the mosque. She looked magnificent, he thought.

"I can't go back," Anil said. His voice cracked, as it often did when he became emotional.

"I know the worries on your mind. Let's get some food from the *chaiwallahs* on the beach. We can sit by the sea, . . . eat and chat".

They waited for a lull in the traffic before crossing Marine Drive and headed towards Chowpatty Beach, joining the crowd on the long path hugging the sea.

The English, sitting back in chauffer-driven cars, took in the evening air and the sunset through the rolled-down windows of their cars.

The public path provided enough anonymity and privacy for Indians to meet with friends, discuss business deals, arrange marriages, and, of course, talk of politics – conversations that the British would consider seditious.

Gandhiji was in town, and there was much speculation about what he would do next. Another march, hunger strike, or *hudtal* to bring the British administration to a standstill? And when would the damn Firangis leave?

"Do you think Ghandiji will win?" Anil asked his sister. "I don't understand this *satygrahi* business . . . How can one win without fighting?"

She rolled her eyes. "All I know is that every time the Mahatma does something, business goes down. Besides, you and I have our own problems, don't we? Let's see what the *chaiwallahs* have to offer."

Bai set a large shawl down on the beach and laid down the plates of kebabs, samosas, *pani puri* and some tamarind juice. Then they both, with unspoken agreement, poked little holes in the puris and carefully filled them with the juice before eating them, relishing the tangy burst of tamarind. They munched the snacks in silence and watched the sun setting in the middle of the crescent-shaped bay.

"Anil, I'm going to miss you," she started.

"I don't want to go back to the farm."

"I know that, *beta,* but Bapa will kill us both if you stay here."

"What is there for me to go back to? Zul will inherit the farm. It's too small to divide."

"I know. You have the brains, but he had the *naseeb* to be the first-born son. That's how it's always been. Bapa has always expected you'd stay with the family on the farm. Besides what would you do here?"

"Can Hussein get me work?"

"Business is bad. These days no one's spending money, especially not on jewellery. Marriage ceremonies are increasingly simple. People even weave their own clothes as Gandhiji asks them to do. Hussein and I survive. But if we squeeze you in, all those *sagawallahs* from his family looking for work will make my life a misery. At least you will have food and shelter on the farm."

"Yes, Zul will feed, house and even clothe me. He's kind, but I'll just end up a *mazdoor*, tilling the land, carrying the harvest to market. He'll give me *hath kharchi* to buy *chai* and *nandi* in the mosque. I'll be one of those helpless men who is treated like boys, told to keep his mouth shut and to say *"Bahut achaa"* to everything.

"But you'll become a *mazdoor* here as well. And where will you live? What are your chances of moving ahead? "

"I'd rather take my chances here. At least I'll be independent, even if it means sleeping on the streets. I would love to sleep on this beach every night. There's more excitement in one day in Mumbai than in a whole year in our village."

Bai looked out at the bay and sat in silence for a few long minutes. Then she turned to Anil and said, "Well, if you're really determined to leave the farm, I may have a better way out."

She pointed to where the sun was setting over the glistening blue Arabian Sea and said, "That's where you should go."

Anil looked at her quizzically.

"To Africa," she said.

She looked at his startled face and continued, "That's your future. So many of my friends have gone and bought shops or farms, or found work on the railways or as clerks for the British. You know for many years our Imam, Mowlana Sultan Mohammed Shah, has been issuing *firmans* to us Ismailis to migrate to Africa. Now the Ismailis have built large *jamatkhannas* in Africa where people can pray and meet freely every day. You won't be alone. When I heard one of his *firmans* a few days ago, still advising us to emigrate, I knew it was a message meant for you. It's your way out."

Anil looked at her dubiously, but she continued.

"Think about it. Here you'll die an old man picking up boxes, trying to save money to go to the cinema, and you'll never read a book. Besides, who will give you a wife? In Africa, you'll have a chance to be somebody. At least you can learn English, perhaps go back to school, and I hear there are lots of good families looking for husbands for their daughters."

Anil tried to imagine what lay on the other side of the ocean. He'd heard talk of the easygoing, tropical city of Mombasa situated on an island near the coast of Kenya.

"I have no money to get there," he said.

"Don't worry about that," said Bai, putting her hand on his shoulder.

They walked back towards Zaveri Bazaar in the cool, moonlit night. By the time they reached home Anil was inclined to agree with her; Africa appeared a far better prospect than farm life as a younger brother in Gujarat.

The next day, after Hussein had gone to work, Bai secretly gave him a package. She told him that it contained her life-savings. She blessed Anil, and gave him a *taweez*, a talisman from a holy man to protect him from evil and disaster.

"But stay at the farm for a few months before you leave," she said.

Back home, he told no one but his mother. When he opened the package he found a simple blue sari and a wad of cash. From then on, a woman in a blue sari would always remind him of his generous sister.

One evening after work, weeks later, he slipped away and boarded an Arab *dhow* at Porbunder bound for Mombasa. It was 1934. He was fourteen and carried few rupees in his pockets, an address in Old Town, and a small, battered bag. He never went back.

****

It was a cool, drizzly July night in Nairobi, thirty years later, when my father first talked about his visit to Mumbai. I had told him the previous night that I'd be going to Kampala to study Math at Makerere College, University of East Africa.

He spoke slowly, with unforgettable sadness, his voice thick, his speech slightly slurred. He'd just finished drinking his daily quota of whiskey, a quarter of Johnny Walker Red Label. He loved his food and drink. When he was at home, he'd start drinking just before sundown, and after a couple of hours of drinking, smoking and reading magazines from India, he would eat a substantial meal, adding a mound of fried green chillies to whatever was on his plate. He had changed from the slim handsome father of my childhood to an enormous, prematurely aged figure. His hair had become silver and his face had turned fleshy, somewhat like his favourite actor Orson Wells.

He worked as a clerk/bookkeeper for a coffee exporting firm, a job whose only redeeming feature was that it paid better than most other clerical work. I always had the sense that he toiled away to provide for his family but he longed to be a free spirit, to lead the life of a wanderer.

When he was in a playful mood, he liked to tell jokes and often at the moment of delivering the punch line, his uncontrollable laughter would sweep you along into happiness. When he simmered with frustration, it would inevitably lead to a shocking outburst of rage.

I wished he had talked about his past earlier. It would have perhaps helped understand his enigmatic and mercurial nature.

That evening he was in an expansive frame of mind. We were sitting in the large main room of our one bedroom flat. It was split into a dining area and a living room with a bed in the corner that he slept on.

"Do you ever feel like going back?" I asked him.

He thought for a bit, looking out at the rain sputtering on the windows and then smiled his crooked smile.

"Not at all. If I'd stayed, I would probably have died by now. I would have worked for my brother or other farmers like a buffalo pushed to do his master's bidding. I would never have travelled and learned English. Never gone elephant hunting, never watched James Mason or Orson Wells, never learned to play bridge. And never tasted good whiskey."

"I've never wanted to go back, never had any regrets," he added, "except one . . . perhaps two."

He showed me the *taweez* his sister had given him. It was a silver pendant strung on a thick black thread.

"I would like to have seen my sister again, just once . . . . but I do have this around my neck. And I often wonder how Mumbai has changed."

Much to my regret, I didn't probe him further; particularly ask him the question "Which village did you come from?"

The past and reconnecting with his family did not seem to matter to him. I admired his courage and ability to live in the present, extracting pleasure daily from a hard life

His last words to me that evening were: "My father snatched away my chance to make something of myself . . .. I know you feel I have not been a good father and you are right in some ways, but remember I have been a much better father than your grandfather was to me. You have the chance of going to college. A degree in Mathematics will help you become a teacher. I hope your children will be doctors, lawyers, or engineers. I don't have much money, but I'll do the best I can to put you through university."

I sensed he had passed on to me the endeavour of fulfilling his dreams.

2. Nairobi, 1974.

It was late afternoon and I was preparing to leave the office a little earlier to get some fresh roses for Najma. It was the anniversary of our first meeting.

On our first date, I had bought flowers for her and put them in the boot of my pale yellow Toyota Corolla. By the time I proudly produced the red roses, they were in severe need of resuscitation. She still laughs every time I give her flowers.

The phone rang.

Mr. Kinyanjui, the head of Treasury Services, wanted to see me. I was acting head of the Computer Department, while John Gregory, the director, was away on vacation. I'd met Mr. K, as he was generally called, only once, so I went up with some trepidation.

It was likely by now that I'd not be able to buy the flowers and probably be late in picking Najma up, but I knew that she would wait patiently, perhaps read or sketch or just sit quietly outside in the front garden of the Aga Khan Academy school where she taught.

Mr. K came out of his office to receive me. He was a tall, slim man in shirtsleeves and red suspenders. With his small moustache under his nose and long Masaai-like face, he was a handsome man. Like me, he was a graduate of London University and had been trained at government expense. He was about ten years older than I. He put his arm around my shoulders in a fatherly way and thanked me for coming.

He offered me a whiskey and we sat down. I could see the construction site for the Kenyatta conference centre, named after the father of the nation Jomo Kenyatta, from where I sat.

Other than being black, Mr. K was the quintessential picture of the smooth, English civil servant. He spoke so softly I had to strain to hear.

"I'll get to the point. According to our newly implemented policy of Africanization, we are looking for someone to replace John Gregory when his contract expires," he said.

John had been treating me as his second-in-command and grooming me to be his successor since I began in the department. Finally, after seven years of hard work, the big promotion was about to be handed to me.

"I think they will be looking for an African," Mr. K said.

He looked at me. I picked up the glass, steadying my hands, and took a sip.

He meant black.

I felt myself turning red, feeling stupid about having assumed for a while that I would be the natural choice.

But I am the most qualified and senior person in the department. Why would they train me in London if they didn't want to promote me? I thought Africanization meant replacing a departing ex-pat with the most qualified citizen. Do you realize I'm a citizen?

I managed to keep the torrent of words running through my mind to myself.

"The Ministry would like you to stay. Your contribution here for the past seven years has been invaluable. But you know that the *Wanainchi* want to see one of their own become the head of the department," Mr. K. continued.

"Thank you for letting me know, sir," I said, hoping I sounded cool and calm.

John, my mentor, had always counseled me to keep a poker face. How ironic I thought, that I am using the British 'stiff upper lip' to prop myself up.

"How do you think we Brits ruled the world for so long?" John often teased. "We never show emotion but quietly plan an attack or tactical withdrawal. Always act normal. Keep surprise on your side till the time comes to use it to your advantage. You Third-Worlders get too emotional."

Mr. K coolly switched the topic of conversation to the work we were doing for his department and began asking details of a number of important projects. I answered with as much detail as I could recall while sipping my drink.

When he finished, he accompanied me to the door.

He lowered his voice, motioned me closer, and said, "It's going to be very difficult for Asians to live here in the long term, especially after what Idi Amin has done. The *Wanainchi* want us to follow General Amin's example and expel all Asians."

Really? I thought. Or do the politicians want to use Amin's mad act to justify their own agenda? To get the masses to think that the Asians are the real problem and to extort money from them for the privilege of being allowed to continue running their businesses.

Perhaps he detected my skepticism. He put his hand on my shoulder and looked at me as if to say, please understand, I have to do this.

In a gentle voice, he said, " You know, I really believe you will do much better in the West."

****

As I drove over to pick up Najma, I recalled a conversation I'd had with George Nderitu over a beer one evening. George, a friend from work, was a Kikuyu who had been educated in the Soviet Union and seemed to have knowledge of decisions being made at higher levels.

I'd not paid much attention to him at the time. But now I clearly saw what he had been getting at.

"I hear Mr. K.'s nephew has just graduated from the States with a degree in computer science," he started out casually.

"Does he want to work in government?"

"Oh, yes."

"We can hire and train him."

"Mr. K. will ask us to do that – they have plans for him."

"What do you mean?"

"He is Mr. K.'s nephew . . . . I wouldn't be surprised if he's destined to run the Computer Department."

"After a few years' experience, and if he is capable."

"Velshi, I know you are probably the most experienced and best qualified to get John's job when he leaves, but Kimathi is a Kikuyu. His father died in the Mau Mau War. He was a commander of the Freedom Fighters and now they have to pay back the debt of his father's sacrifice."

"They?"

"Velshi, you are naïve. I'm talking about the government – the Kikuyu run it like one big family. We may live in the city now, but with the ways of the village. I have land and many goats in the country and yet also a modern flat here. I have a wife in the village and one here, too, as you know. The best of both worlds. Look at you. No wife. Always looking for action."

He laughed and continued, "I can introduce you to Kinyanjui's secretary. She really likes you."

"No. No, thanks."

"Why? You Asians always stick to your own. You'll marry someone of your caste, yes?"

"Hindus do. I am a Muslim. I am not picky that way at all. Colour blind. It's nothing to do with her not being Asian. I think she's very attractive, but I don't like that kind of thing at work."

George raised his hands, smiled, and shook his head

"Tell me more about this Kimathi," I said, filling my glass with the remaining beer.

"Nothing more to add. But let me give you some advice as a friend. Kinyanjui and Kimathi come from the same village. It's our time, we expect the good jobs, be it through merit or connections. We don't have the advantage of money and we don't have the education of our colonial masters' children, but we need to run our own country, even if it isn't done as efficiently as it was in the old days."

"You know I am a citizen, born here not a colonial."

"Of course, Velshi. You are a man with a clean heart. But to most people, you are an Asian, and the British brought the Asians into Kenya. They have never mixed with us and have always supported the Wazungus. True?"

There was no forgiving the whites or us.
"I can't disagree," I mumbled.

George had a bespectacled, professorial look, a laid-back manner, and a drawl. When he stabbed you with a bitter truth, he did it with his wide, beatific smile.

****

That evening, my celebration with Najma at the legendary Norfolk Hotel, where we had first met, was subdued.

I loved the large, stone patio of the sprawling, Tudor-style, two-storied building. The oldest hotel in Nairobi, it was built for the local British aristocracy and wealthy early settlers. It was surrounded by huge, old eucalyptus trees, the remnants of what must have been a large grove, and fenced in by mounds of bougainvillea.

Scattered around us were tables occupied by one of three distinct circles of patrons- black, white and Indians - and only a handful of tables where the groups mixed. These latter groups, still a matter of some curiosity ten years after independence, represented a big shift from the strict segregation we had lived under. The fact that we were now allowed into a place which had been a bastion of colonial power, had given us a great sense of freedom, of being let out of our open-air prisons. But like ex-cons we were still trapped in the old order and felt comfortable in being separate.

What remained of the past, was a few old *Wazungus* in safari suits who still exuded colonial disdain for the rest of us erstwhile subjects of the crown. Thankfully they stuck to darts, billiards, and beer in a space near the bar, leaving the rest of the guests to enjoy the patio.

"You were terribly quiet on that first day we met," I said after we placed our order, a cold Tusker beer for me and a soda water for her.

"Someone had to listen," she said smiling.

My cousin Shehnaz had introduced us. She'd wanted me to meet "this shy girl who writes wonderful poetry" in her literature class.

"Just be a little low key," she had advised me. "Listen more and talk less."

Though Najma said little that evening, I was very much drawn to her quiet self-confidence. I asked her out. The shy girl turned out to be a surprising woman. She talked about herself and her family with utter candour and humour, about her life in an Ismaili colony on the island of Mombasa, the local Aga Khan community schools she had attended and about the neighbours who contributed small sums every month so she could become a *kamadiani*. It was a matter of pride for them that a girl from the colony had been given the honour to lead the student congregation. I envied the strong sense of belonging she had to the close-knit society.

I was disconnected from the community and viewed it with some skepticism. I had given up my British passport, taken up Kenyan citizenship, wanting to become a part of rebuilding a new country, an idealistic and mistaken move. I now had no sense of belonging.

Najma had no interest in politics and a clear sense of identity. Soon we started to go out three or four times a week. My cousin Shehnaz teased me when I went to pick Najma up once, that had she introduced Najma as local *kamadiani* rather than someone who wrote poetry, I would not have shown up at all.

I quizzed Najma on her faith regularly. I suggested that her beliefs sprang from her upbringing just as mine did from my mother who had steered me away from Islam. Najma smiled and patiently rebutted all my points and then if the discussion became prolonged, adroitly changed the subject.

When she told me that her mother was part of the *gusal* committee in Mombasa – volunteer undertakers who prepared bodies for burial, I asked her "Why does your mother volunteer to do that kind of work?"

"She felt that she was contributing to the community in a meaningful way."

It was the start of learning about the community into which I was born and she patiently explained how the

Ismaili community governed itself, the central council that led it, and the myriad of committees under it, challenging my opinion of it as a self-serving bureaucracy.

My mother had kept herself and I away from the community. She felt far more attracted to Hindu philosophy than to Islam and most of her friends were Hindus. My father had little to do with bringing me up. He left that to my mother and in any case he was not around much. When he was, we usually played cards and he taught me gin rummy and bridge, and occasionally he took me to his club where we played billiards and snooker.

Najma's mother was a devout Ismaili who went to the mosque every day for both the early morning and evening services. Najma's father had at one point lost his job as a shipping clerk and her mother had cooked *visi*, catering for families with working wives, and had kept boarders to help pay the bills. He had eventually found a clerical job in a construction company and also kept the books of several small businesses to make ends meet. He, like my father, drank heavily. Najma's parents' marriage, like that of my parents', was a contentious relationship.

Najma's father, however, was an unusual man for his times, a man who loved music and art. He was in great demand as *ginan* singer in the mosque and regularly taught Najma the verses of hymns. After dinner, she reminisced, he would sit with her and talk of grand ships he helped to stock when they docked in Mombasa and the ports of call they berthed at, names that fuelled her dreams of traveling around the world. They sat together and sketched from books on art, discarded from the ships salons, mostly the works of the French Impressionists.

Her main passions were literature and music; she had read voraciously as a child – the Bronte sisters and other nineteenth-century English writers – and had listened to music from old Indian films. Her father taught her to appreciate Indian classical music especially how to recognize the main ragas, a skill that takes years to develop. I was beginning to see that she understood these things at a deeper level than I did.

We were both the first in our families to go to university. She went to the University of East Africa's Nairobi campus and I went to Makerere College in Kampala. Najma's maternal grandparents had, like mine, migrated from the villages of central Gujarat in their early teens, arriving on the *dhows* that carried cargoes of spices, ivory and timber, as well as passengers picked up from Porbunder, Muscat, Oman, and Zanzibar.

We had both received scholarships from the Ismaili Education Department set up by the present Imam, Karim Aga Khan , the grandson of Imam Sultan Mohammed Shah whose advice had prompted my father's immigration.

As we talked, we discovered that we had both escaped from our childhoods into the same songs, books, films and dreams of travel- a train journey across Russia from Vladivostok to Moscow, a journey from Rome to Xian along Marco Polo's Silk Route, taking the Orient Express from Paris to Istanbul or exploring India from the Himalayas to Sri Lanka.

It was her curiosity and simplicity that attracted me. Much later I realized what drew me most to her; she brought much-needed calm into my life.

****

Najma's childhood had its share of poverty and misery but it wasn't, on a day-to-day basis, as chaotic as mine. At least she had lived in the same flat since she was two whereas I had moved more than twenty times by the time I met her. I think it left me with a mixture of restlessness and anxiety but perhaps an ability to adapt to new environments.

When I was old enough to understand, my nanima told me that she had made a terrible mistake in choosing a husband for my mother. Afraid that my mother was destined for spinsterhood after rejecting many suitors, nanima had pressured her daughter, much to her regret, into an arranged marriage.

My mother, who was considered the most educated and learned of the sisters, came from a large rebellious and mostly irreligious family that barely made ends meet. Until my eldest uncle Rajab became a bookmaker for the English horse races and eventually made a fortune that lifted the whole family out of poverty.

My father, a handsome muscular man, was a touch shorter than my mother; a fact that I'm sure bothered him sometimes. My mother, a tall beautiful woman with long black hair and large eyes had opinions that she felt free to share with everyone. The story of my parents' courtship was that my father would stand outside the mosque in Nairobi to admire her and finally submitted an offer of marriage to the family. They met briefly at the mosque and once with a chaperone before they married and settled down in Nairobi. I was born nine months later and at my father's insistence, my mother stopped teaching to look after me.

She never forgave my father for making her stay home, or my grandmother for making the match. The marriage went into a tailspin. My father, driven by the immigrant desire to prove himself, was tortured by his many failures but continued to search for the right new business that would make him wealthy. He had great difficulty in being a reliable provider for the family. To make matters worse, he was addicted to gambling. There were always landlords demanding back rents, rationwallahs reluctant to extend credit for groceries, friends and relatives impatient to be repaid the money they'd lent him. We moved into a succession of single rooms and small flats in Nairobi and briefly to the small town of Eldoret in the White Highlands, where my father tried his hand at running a restaurant.

My mother turned to religion soon after I was born. To the chagrin of my father and my grandmother, she took to Hinduism, back to the religion that we Ismailis were converted from. She even gave me a Hindu name, Manu, ignoring Mehboob (meaning 'the beloved') the name given to me by my oldest aunt, who traditionally was given the honour of choosing the name of her younger sister's children.

According to Hindu mythology, Manu was the first man on earth, the first king to rule this earth, the one who eventually saved mankind from a massive flood, a Hindu version of Adam and Noah, all rolled into one.

No one, including me, knew whether I was a Hindu or a Muslim. My mother became a Krishna *bhakt,* joining one of the major groups of Hinduism and began to read the Geeta to me. The central part of the massive Mahabharata, it is the discourse between Arjun, the mighty warrior, and the Lord Krishna, in which the two discuss the role of duty and the very nature of God, heady stuff for a boy, but as my mother read it to me, I loved the sounds and resonance of the poetry.

Religion was such a central part of life for most Indians, that a sizable amount of time was spent at places of worship, it seemed to me, as family outings.

My father worked near the Jamia Masjid of Nairobi, the main Sunni mosque and sometimes took me there. It was situated near the big McMillan library, in a large compound, with a beautifully maintained garden and fountains, a tranquil place. My impression of Allah was that he was a sombre God, who lived in the quiet and cool space built with marble and filled with calligraphy and mystical designs. Apart from the melody of the muezzin's calls to prayer, he forbade any form of music or any statues. I never saw any women and wondered where they were.

Nanima took my mother and I to the Ismaili mosque for every major celebration. There was a great sense of community. Men and women sat in the same hall, the men in one half, and the women in the other. The service consisted of a few ginans that were sung but never accompanied by music, two short prayers in Gujarati and firmans from the Imam, which were greatly respected and carefully listened to. They addressed the serious subjects of education, women's rights and other social issues. My mother's leaning towards Hinduism had implanted in me a sense of being an outsider in the huge Ismaili family.

My Sikh friends and their parents took me to their Gurdwara. The congregation like the Ismailis sat on the floor in a large hall filled with the fragrance of incense. They had pictures of the Guru Nanak just as Ismailis had pictures of the Imam. The Sikhs were as close-knit a community as Ismailis, bound by a strong faith and familial relationships that went back to villages in Punjab and in our case to Gujarat. In the gurudwaras the central focus was the Guru Granth Sahib, the Sikh religious text. Men covered in white garb from their turbans to their leggings sat cross-legged on a dais and read the shabads from the voluminous Granth. The teachings, verses written in Gurmukhi the Punjabi script, were mostly the work of the first five bhagats, or saints, who had tried to blend Islam and Hinduism. As I looked around the congregation, particularly the tall bearded men in turbans, who carried kirpans sheathed in scabbards covered with sacred geometrical designs, I saw a gathering of magnificent warriors praying to their God for victory in life. The women tall and elegant, in their salawar, kameez and heads draped with chunnis seemed fitting companions to these warriors. I always looked forward to the food offered after the service, the black daal and corn bread.

My mother and her friends took me to Hindu temples full of statues and music and marigolds. The ceremonies were colourful and informal. When members of the congregation entered the temple they announced their presence to the god of their choice by ringing a bell. I was fascinated by the many gods, particularly Hanuman, the monkey god, Kali the fearsome black goddess and Ganesh the half human, half elephant being. Glorious music from bell, cymbals, tablas and harmonium accompanied the beautiful bhajans, poetry written by saints such as Meerabai and Tulsidas. If the Gods were listening, it seemed to me, surely they too would enjoy the music and verses.

My mother became Daulu behen, sister, to all our Hindu neighbours, and I was let into their homes and treated, for all intents and purposes, as a Hindu. I became steeped in the hierarchy in a Hindu culture, the hierarchy in the family and particularly the strictly observed caste system and its many biases.

****

One evening when my father was out at the club, my mother packed up a bag and we took a bus to go to my nanima. This was perhaps the fourth bid to separate from my father and as usual there were many phone calls and attempts at reconciliation but my mother was adamant this time. She started to look for a job after a few weeks at nani's.

We moved into a tenement on Grogan Road on the banks of the Nairobi River. The city was segregated into spacious bungalowed white estates, dense Indian neighbourhoods, and horribly overcrowded black shantytowns.. My mother and I now lived in one of the poorest and most dangerous Indian sections, an industrial area in the valley of the muddy river. While I was relieved from the perpetual anxiety of waiting for the wrong word to be said, one that would erupt into a quarrel between my parents, I now faced another stress, always being on the lookout for goondas who were ready to assault anybody who looked diffident or different.

By this time, I had become acutely aware of the social structure in Kenya. It seemed to me that God had been rigid in assigning roles and authority to people all around me. Everything seemed based on their colour, sex, and age. The colour part was clear-cut. I lived in a separate world occupied only by Indians. The Africans and Europeans had their own worlds, and it was clear that God and the British Government wanted it that way. I knew that the black people fulfilled the role of servants, and were divided into various tribes with much rivalry between them. I knew nothing of the remote white people, except that they lived in beautiful houses and performed the role of managers. We Indians were mostly traders and clerks. It seemed to be accepted by everyone that the Europeans were somehow naturally superior.

In the Indian world, there were many lines that could not be crossed – between the Hindus, the Muslims, the Sikhs, and the Christians, to name only the major ones. They had different customs and cuisines: the Hindus were mostly vegetarians and were horrified by those who ate beef; the Muslims ate meat every day and their men were circumcised; the Sikhs, ate hearty peasant meals, loaded with meats and daal and were people one did not cross; the gentle Christians spoke in strange accents and ate fish on Friday.

I often wondered why God had separated the religions and why transgressions, such as a Hindu girl marrying a Muslim, could lead to beatings, even murder. It became even more complicated when I began to understand that within each religion, there were factions that opposed each other with great ferocity. The Hindu Brahmins, Patels and innumerable castes avoided close contact, especially intermarriage, and the Shia and Sunni Muslims regarded each other as misguided, even dangerous.

I was fascinated by the immense diversity that I witnessed all around me, the religious divisions, the food, the music, the dressing, and perhaps above all the sounds and phrases of the many languages and dialects that were spoken in various neighbourhoods. Urdu had grace and courtliness; Swahili seemed soft and musical; Punjabi had a down-to-earth, peasant like quality; and my own language, Gujarati was practical and businesslike. I learned to read and write in English and Gujarati and could speak the others with different levels of proficiency, picking them up mostly from friends. My mother encouraged me and sometimes demanded that I improve my vocabulary in the language of the "bosses", and reading and using a dictionary became an everyday part of life. Punjabi drew me the most because it had forcefulness and the most satisfyingly vulgar epithets that anyone could enunciate. Knowing Punjabi also gave me the privilege of becoming an honorary Sikh, accepted into their homes and *gurudwaras*.

As we settled into the new neighbourhood, I often wandered through it alone, examining the shops. Grogan Road, named after Colonel Grogan, one of the early powerful English settlers, was a dreary, soulless place, full of carpentry workshops run by Sikhs and desultory ration dukas owned by *banyas* who sold a selection of candies and Indian magazines like *Filmfare* or the more zany *Chakram*. The most lucrative and popular business was the selling of second-hand spare parts, mostly retrieved from stolen cars or vehicles written off in accidents. I remember tall, thin Indian men with dirty fingernails and stained teeth chewing *paan* and smoking endless numbers of cigarettes in ill-lit, cavernous shops whilst their black assistants scurried into the backrooms to bring out requested spare parts.

My mother and I lived on the third floor of a tenement, in a room with a polished, rusty red floor; a single window with bars painted green; and one naked bulb hanging from the middle of the ceiling. The room was furnished with a white metal, double bunk bed, a small table on which we worked, and my mother's solid wood wardrobe, a cherished wedding gift. Our few clothes lay inside it. Books were stacked under the table. We ate in a small six-by-six kitchen-cum-bathroom, sitting on low *patlas*.

Outside our bedroom and kitchen there was no privacy. There were two communal toilets at the far end of the corridor and standing in line outside the toilet, sometimes quite uncomfortably, when someone took their time, was a reminder of our straitened circumstances.

Not infrequently, fights broke out in the tenement between neighbours or within a family. There was a noticeable quiet everywhere except for the shouting, swearing and sometimes blows between the antagonists, while the neighbours listened in with interest or embarrassment.

Though we were the poorest within the extended family, I somehow felt that this was a temporary state, one that my mother convinced me would resolve itself. The extended family was always there to help. Meanwhile she brought in books and fed me my favourite foods-fresh rotis and French toast.

****

A few days after we moved in, our next-door neighbour, the inquisitive Ramaben, called out to me as I passed her flat. She seemed always to be sitting on a *patla,* her blouse and sari barely constraining her enormous tummy and breasts, rolling *puris* that she dropped into a cauldron of boiling oil. The *puris* ballooned and came out hot and mouth watering.

She motioned me to sit down and offered me a fresh *puri* and some yogourt laced with green chillies.

"I've seen you read books. What are you reading?" she demanded.

"*A Tale of Two Cities* by Charles Dickens," I replied. I didn't add that it was an abridged version.

"A *buda* English writer. Very famous, no?" she asked.

"Yes," I said, feeling relieved.

"Arrey Rasik, did you hear?" said Ramaben.

Rasik, a hulking fifteen-year-old with discoloured teeth and a bad case of acne, reluctantly raised himself from a bed in the adjoining room and lumbered in.

"This is how you study, *gudha*. Not lying down on a bed and thinking of God knows what."

Rasik, annoyed at being called an ass, threw me a dirty look.

"And, Manu, where do you get these books from?"

"McMillan Library," I mumbled.

"Oh, the big library for *goras*. Are we Indians allowed to borrow books from there?"

"Yes."

"So take Rasik the next time you go and put some sense into his head."

Rasik looked as if he'd be happy to accompany me – to an alley – and fry me into a puree.

"And, Rasik, from now on, you will act as his brother. You will take care of him. There are too many *goondas* in this neighbourhood. He is a little boy. Understand?"

It was later that I discovered that Rasik was the leader of a large gang of teenagers in the tenement but this did not diminish his fear of his mother and so he grudgingly complied in his role as my guardian.

Each Saturday, we trotted off to the McMillan Library, Rasik chewing *paan,* spitting, smoking Ten Cents, and calling everyone a *bhenchod*, while I carried the books. This accusation of sleeping with one's sister was a common swearword in his limited vocabulary. I furnished him with Superman comics, which he read, sitting in the sun outside the library while I borrowed the books.

I was attacked twice by a rival gang and beaten up and had it not been for the intervention of Ramaben and Rasik, the tenements thugs would probably have seriously assaulted me.

****

Suddenly the newspapers were full of horrifying attacks on white farmers.

In the early part of the century, the settlers had taken over the Kikuyu lands not far from the city and renamed that prized, malaria-free territory "the White Highlands". Soon after their attacks on the farms, militant Kikuyus, the Mau Mau, started to carry out violent robberies in Nairobi, in search of arms and cash to bankroll their war and to terrorize the city-dwelling Europeans and Asians into leaving.

The Indian community with few exceptions, believed the media's portrayal of the movement as being gangs of ruthless terrorists and criminals. There was also the unspoken fear that if the British were dislodged, the Indians, as their supporters, would lose their special status and probably face revenge. The Indians did not mind being second class as long as they remained above the black masses and in any case, segregation seemed to complement the caste system quite naturally.

The terrified city was placed under a curfew. All Africans over sixteen had to carry a kipande on their person, an invisible chain they detested. Anyone not carrying an identity card was usually locked up and faced more serious consequences if they were not employed in Nairobi.

I recall standing by the window most evenings, watching the river shimmer as the sun set and wondering where the Mau Mau would strike next. My mother assured me that our neighbourhood was too poor to be looted. It was rumoured that the Mau Mau often held meetings around forested parts of the river where the police did not dare go. At seven, just after sunset, the news from Cable and Wireless came on. It was of course alarming, as news often tend to be and my stomach would contract into painful knots. Sometimes shots cracked into the quiet night and left me sleepless till morning.

Even Rasik and his gang were confined to their homes. Rasik started to read simplified versions of *Tarzan* and *Zorro,* which he seemed to enjoy immensely. I reported to Ramaben that Rasik was reading the classics. She often sent over her famous purees with a hot potato curry or kheer, a milk and rice pudding.

My mother got me books in Gujarati when I was seven. She initially sent me to a Gujarati primary school where I had barely learned to write in Gujarati when she pulled me out on the advice of my uncle Rajab who advised her that English was going to be far more important than Gujarati. So she began filling me up with English spelling, grammar, and books.

She also introduced me to her own brand of politics. When we passed the New Stanley Hotel on our way back from the cinema and saw the black waiters in immaculate white uniforms serving tea or beer to the white folk, she would mutter, "Who do they think they are? We were writing poetry when they were still in their caves."

She never forgave the British for the long sentences they imposed on Gandhiji and was particularly incensed by Churchill who called Gandhi "a half naked fakir." She was bitter about the Partition, which she felt had been encouraged by the British to leave behind a divided India at independence.

She was furious when the colonial government banned the showing of the Indian film *Jhansi Ki Ranee,* made just as the Mau Mau rebellion was starting. The movie was named after the queen of the Maratha kingdom of Jhansi who fought against the British in the Indian Rebellion of 1857. My mother's teenage idol was Sarojini Naidoo, freedom fighter and poet as well as the first president of the Indian National Congress.

She continued to teach me Indian history. The Moguls were her favourites, particularly Akbar, who married the Hindu princess Jodhabai. She told me stories of the nine brilliant men that Akbar surrounded himself with: poets, philosophers, and musicians, both Hindu and Muslim. Among the most famous were Tansen, the great classical singer and composer of new ragas, and Birbal, philosopher and poet whose works have remained important parts of Indian culture today.

My mother would always read to me before bedtime and her soothing voice would bring in the worlds of *The Fruit seller from Kabul* by Tagore and of Defoe's *Robinson Crusoe*. And always the Geeta. Those words, like Ramaben's food, became antidotes to the menace that filled the air during the curfew. Sunsets filled me with dread for a long time after those violent years, and sometimes, on dark days, even now.

In those years, nanima helped augment my mother's meagre wages. Mother worked as a receptionist at a dispensary in Eastleigh, another poor Indian area on the eastern edge of the city, two long bus rides away from Grogan Road. Her closest, and perhaps only friend, Dolly was a fellow secretary at the dispensary. A single woman in her forties, the heavy-set Dolly was painfully conscious of her rapidly thinning hair.

A big part of my mother's social life was having dinner at Dolly's place or at a kebab and tandoori café near the dispensary. The conversation often turned to Dr Iqbal, one of the doctors at the clinic, for whom Dolly had a crippling, and seemingly unrequited, crush. Even I knew that she stood no chance against the young, beautiful nurse, Savita, who also liked the doctor. Dolly even tried a wig. It was obvious and embarrassing, and I decided that I would never fall in love and subject myself to such humiliation.

****

Nanima finally persuaded my parents to reunite. We moved out of Grogan road and back into Parklands, a middle-class Indian neighbourhood, as my father settled into clerking, but there wasn't much love left in their fractured marriage.

There was enough of a connection though, that into our insanely dysfunctional little world my sister Leila was born. My mother descended into what I suppose is now called postpartum depression. It took her an age to recover from it. My sister arrived into the world as a delicate little bundle and was immediately stricken with a bout of diarrhea that almost killed her. Slowly, she grew into a precocious, pretty child with a pert nose and bright eyes. She took to the books my mother and I brought her. Gradually, I took on the responsibility for her, becoming almost a second father, and anxiously worrying about her upbringing, particularly her education. She developed severe asthma sometime in primary school and I regularly took her to the hospital when she was stricken by an attack.

Without the constant and steadying presence of nanima, I don't know how I would have emerged sane from a disjointed childhood. I spent the huge part of my young life in her home, always welcomed, loved and given wonderful treats. Nanima was a no-nonsense woman with a sharp tongue and a wicked sense of humour.

I have fond memories of Nanima, plump and short, wearing a long frock and a *pachedi* with which she covered her head, taking it off only when she relaxed at home. Her hair, tied in a tight little bun, was regularly dyed with henna. I remember the pale blue soft leather purse that she tucked into her bra and which seemed to contain an inexhaustible amount of money. She also kept a yellow *tasbi* – a rosary – in the purse, and a small tin snuffbox. The surface of the box was painted with delicate violet flowers and when she wanted to relax, she would take a tiny pinch of the snuff, draw it vigorously into each nostril and a few sneezes later, she would blow her nose, rest her head on the back of the chair and smile happily.

Her home was always filled with laughter; delightful meals cooked by her *pishi,* Henry; and music. The home was a large bungalow split into two wings that were mirror images of each other. In one wing my Uncle Amir lived with his wife, Sultan, a delicately beautiful woman who reminded me of Elizabeth Taylor. Nanima and my grandfather lived in the other wing and there was room kept aside for her visiting children and grandchildren. She ruled the roost and my grandfather, a quiet, unobtrusive man, unequivocally accepted her strong will. Her main hobby was pottering around in her little garden.

Nanima's home was my refuge from the madness of my world, the only permanent place in my life. I was treated to the cinema on the weekends I was there, and there was often a card game going on. My lovable Uncle Amir, addicted to cards, would allow me to watch him and his friends playing cards, and invariably I got to collect *suti,* a piece of the pot. Pocket money often came from him and my oldest uncle, Rajab, the patriarch who was always willing to help his younger siblings and their children. A tall serious man who wore tinted glasses, he was a voracious reader and sometimes carried on reading at dinnertime only half listening to other members of the family around the table. Amir my youngest uncle was slim, handsome with an infectious smile and was full of jokes and chatter.

Both men were constant sources of kindness and support in those early years and helped me through school with fees, money for clothes and other necessities.

At home, I escaped into books, the radio, and playing with Leila. By the end of the Mau Mau War, I had become addicted to playing cards, reading, and politics. I suffered, and still do, from insomnia.

I attended a government high school, the Duke of Gloucester. Designated exclusively for Asian boys, it was a sprawling pale yellow structure with a large quadrangle in the middle. There were several small gardens in the compound and huge grounds that accommodated soccer and hockey fields, a running track and four tennis courts. The school was located in the middle of the triangle formed by our old apartment in Grogan road, our then flat in Parklands and my nani's house near the Nairobi museum.

The Duke, as we called it, was probably the best Asian public school of its time and provided an English public school education with prefects, assemblies, and uniforms. An Oxford-educated principal, Sadiq Sahib, who made us sing "God Save the Queen" at regular intervals and promoted a completely English curriculum, ran the school, with judicious use of the cane.

We were taught that the centre of the universe, where Greenwich Mean Time, zero degrees longitude, the Magna Carta, and the Industrial Revolution originated, was a little island called England. It had no resources but plenty of factories, so the British came to Africa and India, built railways and roads, and helped to grow tea, coffee, and cotton on a large scale. Then they took the raw material back home and manufactured things out of them, packaged and sold them, often back to us. At the same time, the *sahibs* saved the Africans from themselves – from cannibalism and other savage customs. We learned about counties like Lancashire and Yorkshire, centres of industry, land of cricketers, and of the great metropolises of Manchester, Liverpool, and London. We knew the names of Henry the Eighth's six wives, the achievements of Queen Elizabeth the First, the voyages of Sir Francis Drake, and, of course, we were immersed in the works of Shakespeare, Dickens, Thomas Hardy, and Rudyard Kipling, and were taught that the history of Africa began with the Berlin Treaty of 1884, when the Europeans divided Africa up and took on the responsibility of jointly uplifting the continent. The great explorers Livingstone and Stanley and Speke came in and "discovered" the source of the Nile and a large lake they named after Queen Victoria. Then missionaries, settlers, railways, hospitals, and schools followed. I remember a boy called Jagdish in our English class who was the white teacher's pet. We named him White man's Burden after Kipling's famous poem.

And now, under Elizabeth the Second, we had become the chosen few to be afforded a good, albeit carefully proscribed education. My admiration for British power and accomplishments, abhorrence of the segregation they imposed and total disregard for other cultures grew into a lifelong love-hate relationship with them.

I finished my final year at the British-run school in 1963, the year in which Kenya became independent. Black students were allowed in a year later.

I headed for Makerere College in Kampala, Uganda, far from home.

3. Kampala, 1965.

From the grim world of fighting for space and survival in Nairobi, I entered a world of Oxford inspired architecture: old, ivy-covered halls of residence; quadrangles with gardens; large dining halls presided over by men at high tables; and cosy lecture rooms, where learning, reading, and passionate discussions about politics were the life-blood of our existence.

Nobody cared whether I attended the lectures or not. I drank prodigiously, went to lectures in literature and philosophy, and barely passed my math courses.
I made my first black friend, Simon Gatundu, a Kikuyu with a sharp sense of humour and a mischievous glint in his eyes.

"Do you know how we became Christians?" he would ask of any new acquaintance.

With great glee he would furnish the confused listener with the answer.

"The missionaries came with bibles in their hands when we had land and goats and drank our own home-brewed beer from gourds. We were slowly enlightened . . . Now we have the bible, and the missionaries and settlers have taken the land to build churches and farms – big, efficient farms – to grow coffee and vegetables and roses for the Europeans. We now wear pants, have jobs, live in townships, pay taxes, and drink bottled beer."

His belly would then shake with laughter. Over many bottles of beer, he told me the reality of the Mau Mau War. In sharp contrast to the media's account of the conflict he explained that less than fifty white settlers had died and over ten thousand Africans had met their end. The population of his entire village had been moved from their fertile farm to scrubland, thrown into detention centres or put to work on white farms. Thousands were brutally tortured. His brother could no longer walk. Most of what I had read in the newspapers at the time had been propaganda, he told me, total propaganda.

"Never, ever believe the press, Velshi," he said.

I was floored by the forgiving nature of the young black Africans I met. I still have not forgiven the British for what occurred one Saturday morning at the Empire Cinema in Nairobi. I'd gone to see *Zorro: The Masked Avenger*.

The only tickets left were on the first line near the screen and in the balcony and so I proceeded upstairs. The manager, a muscular young man with close-cropped blond hair blocked me.

"You wogs just don't know your place."

He escorted me down and I watched the remainder of the film downstairs in the front row, all the time seething with anger. "Wog," I discovered much later, means "Wily Oriental Gentleman." But in a world of wogs and nigs, a wog was by far better off than a nig.

I spent the next two years attending as many philosophy classes as my schedule for math allowed, drinking gallons of beer, and spending many nights at the New life or the Susana Club with its fabulous Congolese music and friendly Bugandan girls.

In my final year, life unraveled. I was drinking too much, hardly sleeping and was suddenly filled with a sense of worthlessness – somehow I was not deserving of all these privileges, all this freedom. I felt like a fraud in the company of my friends. They came mostly from professional or business class families, and as they talked about their families, I stayed quiet or lied.

My third year courses became increasingly complex. Nothing made sense. I ended up with a psychiatrist, a Dr. German, a calm, blond, handsome man. Each fortnight, we talked for an hour; he prescribed antidepressants and sleeping pills. I struggled and failed my final year.

Shattered, I went back to Nairobi and began teaching at a private commercial college that accepted teachers with any post secondary school education. Six months and several chats later, my Uncle Rajab persuaded me to return to Makerere and lent me enough money to finish my degree. Most of my college friends had moved on. Most of them were working and occasionally took me out but I was too busy or embarrassed to socialize often. I was driven by the words of my mother and Uncle Rajab - "Finish your studies, Manu--we know you can do it. There is nobody with a college degree in our family."

I worked through the darkest period of my life, studying the whole day and running every evening until I was ready to drop. At night I drank one beer and slept a few hours. I clawed my way out of depression, completed my degree and rejoined the real world. I found myself unemployed, with teaching Mathematics, probably in a small, provincial town as the only possible career to follow.

Then one of those moments of serendipity that transforms life came to pass.

A friend suggested I take a test in something called Computer Programming. The Ministry of Finance was looking for programmers and was carrying out aptitude testing of recent graduates. I passed the test with apparently record-breaking scores. All those years of logic, numbers and algebra must have paid off.

The Ministry offered me a job and I embarked on what became a lifelong career. I loved the creative work and put in long hours. It was a time of great optimism and hope in the country. I felt proud of being part of the great project of building a new independent nation, a project that almost all Kenyans felt engaged in.

****

After two years, I was chosen by the government to pursue graduate studies in Computer science at London University, on the understanding that I would be fast-tracked to a senior civil servant position in the Ministry upon my return.

I was awed by the city of London. The computer field was just beginning to be taught in universities and some of the courses were extremely theoretical and of little practical value but it gave me a powerful insight into just how the industry was developing.

I met a beautiful blond girl from Canada and had my first serious affair. Joni and I both loved the city, with its varied architecture, complex history, and vibrant nightlife. Sometimes we went to Oxford and wandered through its colleges and pubs.

I remember taking her to listen to a sitar concert by Ravi Shankar at the Royal Albert Hall. She sat frozen and frustrated with the music while I was entranced. It was one of many things which was to underline the differences in our backgrounds.

After eighteen months in London, I came back to Nairobi, and slowly lost touch with Joni. My career took off, and I had my own apartment and a car, a sporty Toyota. I had almost everything I could wish for but still suffered from bouts of depression. By this time my parents had moved to Mombasa and I occasionally drove down for weekend visits.

I met Najma, a few months after my return from London. She became the first person with whom I shared the painful memories of my childhood with complete honesty, mainly because she never hid anything.

Najma's childhood had forged patience, discipline, calm, and, above all, an unshakeable faith in religion. I was different in every way, an impatient and mercurial rebel, with no faith in a personal God. I am six feet tall and she is five. She understood my moods. Our dating was as much about sharing our pasts as courting. In a short time, we became confessors and confidantes.

We were married within six months and rented a very small townhouse in Karen, a suburb of Nairobi named after the writer Karen Blixen. We had a quiet, idyllic life there. I often read in our front yard, sitting on a bench under the single tree – a lush mimosa, with yellow flowers. But after a life of living in small flats and tenements, I felt like an outsider, a trespasser. Marriage had been the start of a life so different from the one I'd lived that when old memories came back, I occasionally drove through the old neighbourhood of Grogan Road, in part to feel a sense of familiarity and to realize how fortunate I had been to escape that life.

Slowly I began to appreciate the other Kenya, the European one, the one with gardens, space, and privilege. But then, just when I thought my life was finally settled, Mr. K. called me into his office.

****

We sat quietly at the Norfolk watching the sunset for quite a while. Lost in the memories of the past, I suddenly realized it was getting dark and the patio was filled up. We each ordered a steak dinner and I had a glass of wine.

"You know, we may have to leave Kenya," I said to Najma.

"Well, a lot of people are leaving. And so can we. Think of how far we've come. Did you ever think we could afford to eat at a place like this – even be allowed to sit here? We can go to England, Canada, or even America."

It had been two years since Idi Amin made the announcement ordering Asians including citizens out of Uganda. Like most Asians in Kenya and Tanzania we had followed what was happening in Uganda with horror and disbelief. Amin had cancelled their Ugandan passports, frozen their assets, other than an allowance of fifty pounds to take out of the country. He gave them ninety days to leave.

The stateless Asians scrambled to get visas and tickets to get out. The army or civil servants grabbed their homes and businesses as they left. Cars were left at the airport or given to servants. The army or customs officials stripped those found trying to smuggle out jewellery or foreign currency. Amin often personally supervised their departure at the Entebbe airport.

Since the governments of the three most popular destinations, the U.K, the US and Canada had issued limited entry visas, many were forced into UN refugee camps or other countries that would accept them. These events prompted the majority of Asians in Kenya and Tanzania to begin planning their own exits and those who could do, started moving their assets out of the country.

Najma and I were afraid that our parents would not survive that kind of ordeal, and this further motivated us to leave Kenya to establish a base from where we could sponsor them if the worst-case scenario happened. In retrospect, the Asians turned out to have had a lucky escape as Amin ruthlessly murdered thousands of his fellow countrymen in the quest to establish, and propagate, his insane dictatorship.

****

Though logic dictated that we should leave, we went through weeks of angst deciding whether to leave or stay. Looking for advice, we talked to our friends in Nairobi. They were divided into two main camps with strong opposing views.

One group, like us, was worried that we could face deportation as the Ugandan Asians had and if not, crime, corruption, and antipathy towards us would eventually make life simply too difficult and dangerous.

The other camp recognized the danger of continuing to live in Kenya but argued strongly that the rewards outweighed the risks.

"Look here, this is a new country. Things will sort themselves out. In the meantime, we have a wonderful climate and servants to do everything. This government will never throw us out – we're the goose that lays the golden egg. We give them shares in our companies, directorships, *paisa* for licenses. You want to go to Canada or the U.K., live in cold winters, do your own cleaning and laundry and be called Pakis? Just move back into our Indian areas. We have security guards and dogs; we're putting in electric fences. There's crime everywhere in the world. Have you read about Chicago? Besides, you know, we will run this country for decades . . . These people have to learn to run a country. Many have just come from villages, seen cars for the first time. Just go with the flow. So what if they want *baksheesh*. We make enough money to share with them."

Finally, Najma helped crystallize my angst into a decision.

"We can't live here in fear of being expelled by the government, continually worry about being robbed or attacked. We know we're resented. Do we want to bring up our children here? What future will they have? We've always dreamed of travelling so let's treat this as our first big trip and adventure. We can always come back if things don't work out. You choose the country. I'll start planning. We'll need to pack, give notices to the landlord, fill out visa applications. There'll be much to do."

With my computer skills, I felt I had options. It was a choice between Britain, Canada and the U.S. Where would we fit in best and find the most acceptance?

The British government under Ted Heath had tried every means to keep Asians out of Britain and reluctantly accepted those who had British passports. I had seen enough xenophobic headlines in newspapers about the 'Asian invasion' to realize we were not welcome.

Did I want to live in the U.S.? I had followed the bitter battle for civil rights throughout the sixties and after Martin Luther King was assassinated in 1968, I began to feel that his dream of an America free of segregation and racism was not going to happen anytime soon. Apart from that, the war in Vietnam and American support of dictators particularly in South America and Africa reminded me of British imperialism during colonial times. A more sophisticated form but nonetheless, imperialism. I felt I would not feel comfortable living in a society that waged war and continued to grapple with prejudice.

The man I admired the most was young, charismatic, and liberal: Pierre Trudeau, the Prime Minister of Canada. He had opened the doors of immigration to people around the world based on what they had to offer, not on where they came from. A large number of Ismailis who fled from Uganda were airlifted in planes sent by the Aga Khan and flown to Montreal, where they were given help in settling down, making Trudeau a hero in East Africa.

I concluded that the country that had elected a man like Trudeau was where we should go.   I've never had cause to regret it.

****

Soon after we were granted visas for Canada, we drove to Mombasa where both sets of our parents now lived. We spent out first evening with Najma's parents.

Najma's parents who had wanted their three daughters to leave Kenya and settle down in the West were delighted when we told them our plans to emigrate. Her sister Shehnaz had a boyfriend in Texas, a childhood sweetheart and Nilu's boyfriend Mukesh was planning to move to the U.K for business.

I sat with Najma's father drinking beer while her mother prepared mishkaki (barbecued beef cubes)- and red snapper cooked in masala. A small tape recorder played a mixture of popular songs from the fifties and some semi-classical music.

The conversation drifted to the earlier migrations. Najma's grandparents had come from around the same group of villages in India as my family, around the cities of Rajkot and Manjevdi. Both Najma's parents were born in Africa, her father in Mombasa and her mother on a farm on the foothills of Mount Kilimanjaro. Kulsumbai talked of her life on the farm her parents had carved out from the bush. One of her major duties was to help her father look after the cattle and supervise the itinerant workers, Chagga tribesmen. She had to learn to repair the family Bedford truck, and to handle a gun and occasionally use it to scare off lions that wanted to drag off a cow or a calf. Najma's father revealed that he had left school at fourteen to look after his family after his father's business had failed.

I silently watched the family as they talked. They were all short, around five feet. Najma's mother was dark, wore spectacles and looked muscular, whilst her father was fair, plump with a regal face. The girls were unmistakably sisters. It struck me how strong the family was and it was clear from where Najma had inherited both her stoicism and her unwavering spirituality.

The next day we visited my parents. My sister, Leila, had grown into a strikingly beautiful young woman, tall, slim and in many ways resembled my mother. I was particularly happy that Najma and Leila got along well, planning their shopping and seeming to exchange confidences.

That evening, my mother cooked my favourite meal, a chicken curry, with homemade chapattis and samosas. My father, as usual, drank too much. Before dinner, he sat with Najma and Leila to give them a lesson in bridge, a game he played superbly, whilst I chatted with my mother in the kitchen.

My mother stopped after taking the samosas out of the oven, took my hand in hers, and asked very softly, "Is everything okay with you? Are you *sukhi?*" Knowing how wary of marriage I had been, she wanted reassurance that I was happy with Najma.

"Ma, it's been wonderful so far. We don't disagree on much. She goes to the mosque often. It gives her great peace and sometimes she even gets me to accompany her. She calls me 'Mehboob,' not 'Manu,' " I teased my mother. Towards the end of her life, she had come to appreciate the Ismaili emphasis on educating women, appointing them as leaders, and removing dressing restrictions. But I knew that, at heart, she remained a Hindu.

The once tall, strong-willed feminist was now thin, hunched, and often disoriented. As a child, I often had the sense that I was watching a beautiful and bright bird, living in a cage. More than the constant moving, the poverty, the fear during Mau Mau days, or any other misery, my greatest pain was seeing her struggle between wanting to leave the man she never loved and staying with the boy she couldn't leave. And I felt responsible for her imprisonment.

She extracted a promise from me: "Look after Leila. She is bright and will soon go to university. I want you to make sure she is looked after. She respects you, and I know she's angry with me because I have not been a good mother to her. You know I have suffered from depression for years."

During dinner, we joked a lot and overate and finally over dessert, we gave them the news. There was a short, surprised silence.

"But you've just got married. Why do you want to leave so soon?" my father asked as he took a long drag from his cigarette.

I told them about my conversation with Mr. Kinyanjui.

"Let's face it," my mother said, "we sided with the British and treated the blacks terribly. We are racists. We stood by when they fought for independence. There is no Gandhi here; they won't forgive us. Better to go. The sooner the better."

"The blacks will never run this country by themselves," my father countered. "They'll need people like you. Let them put up figureheads as bosses. What do you care?"

"You are the kind of person they are mad at. People who think they can't rule themselves," my mother replied exasperated

My father burst out laughing and said, "I could have gone back to India and married a simple *desi* woman who would have never argued with me and got a good dowry. Instead, what did I do? I married Jhansi ki Rani.

It was a good time to step in. "We've got our papers and we'll be leaving in two months. We just wanted to tell you that after we settle in, and if there is trouble here, we could sponsor you."

My father smiled and said quietly, "It is now exactly forty years since I immigrated. One big move in a lifetime is enough. I will live out my days here."

My mother turned to me and said, "You know the doctors have told him to stop drinking. He's already had three heart attacks. Talk some sense into him. He's only fifty-four."

My father continued to smile, dismissing her plea. Now, when he had run out of rage, my mother was showing much greater care and concern for him.

"Well, hopefully you can come one summer after we're settled," I said. "And I want you to know that when you retire, we'll be sending money to make sure you're comfortable."

"I'd like to come to Canada after you're settled and go to university there," Leila said, her eyes pleading

"We'll come when you get your first born," my mother said with a glimmer of hope.

I never saw my father again. He died after his next heart attack two years later.

II.   CANADA

"When in the end, the day came on which I was going away, I learned the strange learning that things can happen which we ourselves cannot possibly imagine, either beforehand, or at the time when they are taking place, or afterwards when we look back at them."

Out of Africa by Isak Dinesan.

4. Toronto, 1974.

We landed in a city with streets covered in snow, trees bare of leaves, its sky grey. It was a shocking contrast to Nairobi's towering eucalypti, green lawns and bougainvillea covered in brilliant sunshine.

As we left the aircraft we bid farewell to a motherly airhostess who had stopped to chat to us a few times during the flight and somehow made me feel that in choosing Air Canada I had taken a small step towards becoming Canadian. If everybody was as friendly as the airhostess then we had nothing to fear.

The immigration line was long and led me to imagine all kinds of potential problems with our papers. The level of my anxiety rose as the slow and deliberate immigration officer examined our pink landed immigrant papers, and asked us questions the answers to which lay on the papers. Finally, he smiled slightly, welcomed us solemnly, stamped the papers, and told us to go apply for our social insurance numbers and medical insurance. We walked out feeling almost like citizens.

Outside, there was no sign of Shiraz, my cousin. We had planned to stay with him till we found jobs. We waited with mounting concern and were thinking of getting a taxi when our names were announced on the PA. Anxious and worried, we reported to the announcements desk.

Two strangers were waiting for us. They introduced themselves as Sadat and Fatima, friends of Shiraz, and explained that he could not meet us as he was attending a training course. Unfortunately, Shiraz had another friend and his family staying with him and the superintendant of the building was threatening to throw them all out.

"Not to worry, they've found another place for you to stay," said the calm and smiling Fatima.

We chatted as we drove into the city. I noticed how confident and settled they both seemed, unruffled by the traffic on the enormous eight-lane highway, strangely named the 401. Would I ever drive as comfortably as Sadat, I asked myself?

They dropped us off at a rooming house on Yonge Street managed by a busy and polite young Ismaili. After he showed us the laundry and the TV lounge, he informed us of the daily rate, a hundred dollars a week. We made our way to our room, a small dark space in the basement, a place that immediately assailed me with claustrophobia and dejection.

We sat on the bed and looked at our bags.

Everything we possessed lay on our persons or in the bags. Our nest egg consisted of $900 raised mostly through the sale of our most prized possession, the Toyota Corolla. Our greatest assets were our professions, our ability to speak English, and thirty LPs we'd collected over several years.

"Shall we unpack?" I asked Najma.

"No, let's go out for fresh air. Maybe we can find a map of the city and figure out where we are."

Najma unpacked the coat she had bought in London. We had been told that Canadian coats were bulky and ugly and the coats from London were smartly fashionable and lasted longer. The British could still make some things better than anybody. We had gone into a small boutique in Oxford Circus and asked for help in making the right choice. A kindly, bespectacled old lady had looked at Najma and turned to me.

" Does the little lady speak English?" she asked.

I looked at her nonplussed and then slowly replied, " Actually, she teaches English."

The lady seemed to go into a flutter, recovered and finally said, "That will make it easy won't it, dear."

The little lady coat had become a private joke between us.

Najma put it on as we headed out to Yonge Street

Watching Dr. Zhivago at the Nairobi drive-in cinema I had been awed by the beauty of the snow but nothing had prepared me for the assault of the cold air on my senses. The coats and jackets might as well have not been there.

Eyes watering, noses dripping, we trudged through the snow on the busy thoroughfare till we came upon a subway station called Lawrence where we picked up a map.

Najma, the geographer said, "I suppose these streets like Lawrence, where we are and York Mills must run east west and these one like Pape and Chester north to south. So it's a grid."

We walked a little north, stopping outside a hamburger restaurant and looked at the price. Two dollars for a burger and chips with a drink was converted to twenty shilling, forty for two, an outrageous price to us. We bought three doughnuts and munched them on the way back.

Homesickness shot through me. I missed Nairobi, its Sunday afternoon beers and a curry lunch on a patio in the company of friends. I did a quick calculation and told Najma that accounting for the rent, transport and food at these exorbitant prices and some pocket money, we'd run out of money in five or six weeks if we didn't get a job.

Najma thought for a bit and said, "My best friend Shemina's brother, Sadru had come to Mombasa and he'd invited us to stay with him for a few days, if we needed a place."

She took out her little black book and we figured out how to make a phone call from a pay station. Sadru sounded pleased to hear from us and invited us to stay with him for a week. He had someone else coming in afterwards.

God bless him, he arrived to collect us within the hour.

Sheepishly, we approached the rooming house manager and explained that we could not afford to stay there.

He smiled and said, "Better to let me know now than not pay me later."

Sadru drove us to his home, near the airport where his wife Zareen had cooked a wonderful chicken curry. We sat up late, chatted about the good old days in Kenya and Sadru, an accountant in Africa, told us about his job in a warehouse.

"I have this wonderful little truck with a forklift," he said smiling wryly, "and we have managed a down payment on this townhouse. We are happy, Canada is a wonderful place, awfully cold but safe."

We went to bed comfortable under a duvet. It was still snowing outside.

Over the next few days we got our social security numbers, registered for health insurance, and started looking at newspaper ads for jobs. Najma managed to locate Alim, who was her Jamatbhai, in charge of administration, like a deacon, when she was the Kamadiani, presiding over the ceremonies at the university mosque. He was delighted to hear from her and said he had room to put us up and adding, half jokingly, that she would have to cook for the men sharing the apartment, all of whom she knew from her college days.

And so we entered the world of four men who still remain close friends to this day.

Najma introduced me to Jaffer, Hussein, Mo and Alim, all of whom treated her like a younger sister, who had married a roguish character. Most of her friends who were mosque-going teetotalers knew that I drank and rarely prayed.

That evening Najma cooked a light chicken biriyani, with mounds of yellow rice, accompanied by a pungent salad of onions, chillies, tomatoes and cucumber in vinegar and raita, yogurt full of garlic and cucumbers to cool things off. I went through a litre of cheap wine and smoked incessantly as I listened to the four men's stories of migration to Canada.

Hussein, made stateless by the mad general Amin, had been shuttled back and forth, a refugee hot potato, by immigration officers in Kenya and the UK. After having lived in the airport for a week, a British immigration officer took pity on him and gave him a three-month visa to stay in England while applying to come to Canada.

Alim and Jaffer had left Tanzania with ten pounds in their pockets, landed in London, quickly set up a stall to sell jeans for a merchant in London's West End and collected enough money for a passage to Canada.

Mo was a student on scholarship for his Masters in mechanical engineering.

They told their tales with humour, were obviously bright, articulate, and quite unperturbed by the fact that they were practically broke and depended on each other's help for survival. In their dealings there was no accounting for money or fuss, just generosity and empathy. Over Christmas they helped us with our resumes, coached us on how to answer questions- never be humble, tell an employer you can handle anything, you'll find you are more than able to and don't get awed by your colleagues' versions of their own abilities.

Najma was the first to get a job. It was a data entry position at a medical clinic, near Parliament Street, processing a daily quota of medical insurance claims for doctors working at the centre. She did the mindless job without complaint, just about managing to finish her quota each evening. She soon discovered the area was a favourite haunt for ladies of the night and in the early days the johns looking for hookers when she left work pestered her. She soon learned to laugh at their propositioning.

I began to learn to cook a reasonable curry. As I tried to do the tasks that had traditionally been done by servants in Kenya, I began to appreciate how difficult and tiresome being a house servant must have been and how unsympathetic the Indians and Whites must have appeared towards the work the Africans were forced to do.

Whilst we knew that racism was not condoned or institutionalized in the city, there were quite a few occasions when we were out walking, that some young person, would roll the windows of the car down and yell "Paki, go home". We did meet Canadians who were clearly uncomfortable with outsiders like us but everyone was polite, sometimes maddeningly so. We also met many Canadians who were friendly, sympathetic and sometimes even apologetic. Most of us were just thankful that corruption, fear of the police and segregation were not part of the city's social fabric.

Our entertainment on the weekend was often going to the mosque, getting *nandi* and having it as TV dinner whilst watching *Perry Mason* or the *Streets of San Francisco*. Occasionally we went to MacDonald's for a burger or the Ponderosa for a steak.

It was a far cry from the nightlife of Nairobi-- the late night drinks at the Hilton or the visits to the Nairobi Casino to play blackjack or just to watch the smooth French croupiers in action. When the wind stung my face as I waited for a bus on a wintry day or the sunset arrived at 4pm after a short dreary day, I remembered my zippy Toyota, its windows rolled down to let in cool air on a glorious sunny day.

I reminded myself of all the reasons why I had come to this cold and difficult country and sometimes when I was ready to go back, my pride grew fierce and shook its head adamantly.

I got a job as an analyst at a Trust company earning three hundred dollars a week. Information about salaries was freely exchanged between friends and I was considered the best paid. We saved enough money to buy a used car and to make a down payment on a condo in Scarborough under a government assisted first time buyer program.

We sponsored my sister Leila and took out a loan to send her to an expensive private girls school in Toronto. Najma also went back to teachers college to get her teaching certificate.

We felt we had achieved a great deal in the first two years of our life in Canada.

Then I received news that my father had passed away. I could not afford to go back for his funeral and focused on arranging my mother's affairs from a distance. With the help of Najma's mother and Moni, a close friend of mine, we managed to get the few assets sold, paid off any outstanding debts and had her looked after till she got her papers to immigrate.

My career took off and work began to consume me. Whenever I was at home, which was not often, I sensed the stress facing the three women cooped in the small apartment. My mother helped with the cooking but had no friends, hated the winter and was not confident enough to go out on her own. My sister had entered the University of Toronto. She had to share a small room with my mother and had few resources to enjoy her university life. Najma received her teaching certificate and managed to get one interview for a teaching job with two hundred applicants. She struggled through a succession of clerical and accounting jobs. She was finally pregnant after suffering two miscarriages.

I was overwhelmed with the responsibilities for the growing family and had little time and sympathy for anyone. We could, however, finally afford to buy a little semi-detached bungalow that could house the growing family. There was more space, a basement apartment for my mother and sister and even a separate room for the baby. I prepared for a great deal more stress in my life with another soul to worry about.

But instead, a beautiful and ever smiling boy entered our lives and brought pure joy and suddenly my daily troubles seemed much less important. We named him Abid.

5. Toronto, 2005.

"I have found my first full-time job, Dad It's in Mumbai." Abid announced.

I had spent weeks watching him hunched over a computer in our basement and had been worrying about how he was going to join the workforce after finishing his degree.

"You mean like in Mumbai, India?"
"Yes," he replied testily.

Abid is a man of few words.

"So . . . what's the job, who with?"

He is a handsome young man with large eyes that light up when he smiles. His usual T-shirt and jeans, the unofficial uniform of Canadian youth, make him look leaner than he is. He reached out and put his hand on my arm.

" You'll be pleased. It's a programming internship, Dad. They don't pay much but enough to live on. It's with TCS. I start in three weeks in Mumbai and they send you for training and then at least a year on a project."

I knew a little about TCS, Tata Consulting Services, an Indian outsourcing giant that employed over fifty thousand computer consultants and operated globally.

"That's a pretty good company, but do you know much about Mumbai?"

"Well, I've read a lot about Mumbai and Calcutta. Calcutta is tougher than Mumbai – at least that's where all the ex-pats go. I know it's overcrowded."

I thought to myself, you can't possibly understand overcrowding.

We were sitting on our deck, looking out to the large backyard with its three towering trees – two Norwegian spruces and a beech. At the height of the fall, the beech stood like a huge cone of golden yellow leaves rustling in the early evening breeze. Our side-split home had three bedrooms, a large family room, and a basement apartment that Abid had claimed as his pad. In Mumbai, you could not get this much land except possibly in one or two super-elite enclaves. And it would cost millions. A dozen or more average Indians could, and would, gladly fit into our house.

"Mumbai has a population of twenty million people, unofficially," I said. "That's Toronto, Montreal, and Vancouver put together and then some. My guess is that it's about half the size of Toronto in terms of area, and half the city lives in slums," I said realizing I was in lecture mode.

Najma popped her head out through the patio doorway.

" Here is a plate of potato fritters. They're hot, I just made them."

After placing the plate on the table, she looked at us and said, " What's the matter, why aren't you eating, usually you just grab them …what's going on?"

I asked her to sit down, and Abid told her the news.

"Why India, Abid?" she asked.

"I want to do something out of the box."

"Out of the box?"

"You know, we've lived this comfortable middle-class life in this nice house in this nice suburb, and don't get me wrong, I'm grateful, but I need a change from designer clothes and clubbing and all that. I don't want to settle down here, at least not without travelling."

Najma and I looked at each other and smiled. We worked so damn hard to give him this middle-class life. Apart from years of saving to pay off the mortgage, there was the work we put into the house. The backyard was a labour of love, particularly for Najma – years of work to grow and build a rose garden, maintain a small pond with lilies, nurture Japanese maples, and mow a lush lawn. And we'd finally built a deck painted periwinkle blue, as Najma had suggested. It had become our favourite space in the summer.

I saw this piece of land through the eyes of the proverbial penniless immigrant who had achieved his dream. For Abid, though, this backyard was where he'd played most of his life, and now he'd outgrown it. He had to discover other worlds.

Sameena slunk into the backyard. She'd been out playing soccer. She was a sports fan – played hockey and soccer and socialized too much. But her grades were high; I had no grounds for protest. With her mass of curly hair and a gift of mimicry and repartee, she always managed to make us laugh. She had been born in this house and had never known the adversities we had faced.

"So he told you, eh?" she grinned, taking off her Adidas and flopping down on the chair beside Abid.

She savoured the moment of having been the sole confidante.

"You should have heard them when he was booking a hotel room," she said.

"What is your good name, sir?" She put on her very credible Indian accent.

"How can a name be good or bad?" she asked me.

"Actually, 'good' is a substitute for subh . . . meaning 'propitious.'"

"Propitious??"

"Yes, something that bodes well for the future . . . Hindu parents usually get the name from a *jyotishi,* a holy man who reads astrological charts and chooses the name."

"So the name is chosen for a good future? How do you get introduced to girls you want to date? This young man's good name is Abid?" she said, breaking into peals of laughter.

"By the way, they still use the astrologers – even the politicians and big businessmen – for marriages, for a lot of important events," I added.

"Abid," I went on, "do you realize how different life will be? You speak only English, your favourite food is Japanese, your favourite sport is hockey, and you think Indian movies are corny, hilarious. You're going to get curry morning, noon, and dinner, and life will revolve around cricket – more than hockey and baseball put together. Everyone knows Sachin Tendulkar – he is a god – but nobody's heard of Sydney Crosby. And everyone loves Bollywood."

"Stop teasing him, you two," Najma intervened. "Do you have enough money, Abid?"

"I've saved some money, and I have a ten thousand dollar line of credit and my Visa and debit cards. We have a meeting in Mumbai on Monday. I've booked a hotel in Colaba. That's where the offices are."

" So he's fine, " Najma said looking at me

"Dad," Abid continued, "how often have you said we have no idea of how the other half lives. You went to India in . . . when was it? '92? I thought you said it was unforgettable."

I nodded. Yes, it was unforgettable. We'd given them exciting accounts of our trip, of unpredictable India but we'd never told them much about the riots we'd got caught up in.

"Let's face it, you are really very Indian," Abid went on. "We still eat Indian food and you listen to that weird music. You and mum often talk in Gujarati. You've always talked about searching for your father's family. I can make some inquiries. Maybe you can come over later and we can go to Gujarat together. I really would like that."

"What a great idea," Sameena piped up, "we should all go to see Abid this winter. Sabrina's just come back from Goa. She said the beaches are to die for, and there's lobster and shrimp curry, and massages on the beach. They paid ten dollars for a shack. We could stay in a shack and save you money, Dad."

Najma took their side and looked at me "You hate the winter. Let's take Sameena and visit Abid."

"It'll really be great. I'll have figured out where to stay. We don't have to do four-star hotels. It'll be fun," Abid beamed.

Suddenly, Abid's new job had produced a family trip. Najma, Abid and Sameena took the snacks and glasses off the table and went in.

At the end of a long Canadian summer day, when the sun starts to set and I'm left alone, I often think of my mother reading to me at the start of curfew time in that one room with the rusty red floor on Grogan road.

This time, I thought of my father and sister as well.

After about six years of living with me, my mother had moved into a seniors' home and begun to enjoy her independence. She was getting government assistance, felt free to do as she chose, went regularly to a library, kept a journal and volunteered helping her neighbours deal with government letters and forms in English. She was happier than I had seen her in years.

Leila had graduated and moved out.

We all continued to meet regularly until, a few years later, I began to see disturbing changes in my mother. She had, the doctor told me, developed dementia. The children giggled when she couldn't remember their names. I was the only person whose name she remembered.

Leila came to visit us less frequently. We seemed to get into an argument whenever we met and lost our closeness. I discovered eventually that she had developed a form of painful arthritis, possibly rheumatoid, and sometimes could barely walk.

When it became clear that my mother had little time left, I took Leila to visit her. My mother did not remember who she was. Leila was devastated by what she interpreted as a final show of her mother's disinterest and it was the last time they met.

Leila and I became estranged and have completely lost touch. Since coming to Canada this has become my most painful loss, one that has, over time not become any easier to bear.

Before my mother died she said to me, " My biggest joy has been to play with my grandchildren. I wish your father could have seen his grandchildren."

I wished that too but at least now my father's and Abid's journeys were going to cross paths. Abid's hotel in Colaba was within walking distance of Chowpatty Beach, where my father's sister took him one evening for a walk and pointed towards the east coast of Africa. That evening had started a remarkable journey for my family – to Africa, then Canada and now back to the starting point in Mumbai.

I tried to imagine how my father, as a fourteen-year-old boy who spoke only Gujarati, must have felt during the month he was travelling across the Indian Ocean in the cramped hold of a dhow, its huge triangular sail pushed by the monsoon winds, as he guarded the small stash of rupees that were to be his only means of survival to begin with. Once he arrived in Mombasa, he'd ended up working as a stock boy for an Indian trader and slept in the warehouse. He'd taught himself enough about accounting to become the trader's bookkeeper.

Abid's journey would start with his credit card, a laptop computer and an internship with a global computer-consulting outfit waiting for him upon arrival.

Both my children and my father have one thing in common: a strong sense of identity and self-assurance.

My father loved Gujarati peasant food and cricket, arguing and debating, and melodramatic Indian films. He saw himself as an Indian. A creature of his time, he believed that women existed to cook and bear and rear children properly – to be quiet and obedient.

My children, products of a new multicultural generation, rarely see themselves in terms of race or colour. They are far more interested in the environment than religion. They enjoy hockey and baseball, listen to rap music, and prefer Japanese, Italian, and other cuisines to Indian food. They have a strong sense of belonging. Their childhood memories are of growing up in Toronto in a stable, middle-class environment, and they see themselves simply as Canadians.

Life is much simpler, I imagine if you are born in a country where you feel you belong, you speak a single language and a passport is just a document that allows you to travel.

I cannot define myself with that kind of clarity. My most powerful memories are of an African childhood, my favourite food and music comes from the subcontinent of India, I think in English, I was born an Ismaili and brought up as both a Muslim and a Hindu. I gave up my British passport and then my Kenyan citizenship to become a Canadian. Each nationality change was like a divorce and remarriage, accompanied by emotional upheaval, time-consuming legal paperwork, and new vows of loyalty.

During my first trip to India, I felt completely at home. I even came to appreciate the bright, loud, sometimes gaudy and garish colours – of clothes and houses, of the spices and food. Whenever I spoke Hindi or another Indian language, more often than not, a smile appeared, an instant bond was established, family matters were brought up, advice was sought. Sometimes, an invitation for a meal was even extended. I was no longer a tourist but an Indian who had done well. I felt I belonged.

India grabs you. For so many people the struggle for livelihood is so powerful that it's impossible to remain detached from it. Some visitors just can't take the seeming wretchedness, and swear never to return. Others accept the reality and perhaps get glimpses of the Indian acceptance of life and even optimism and the willingness to shape lives out of the struggle for survival.

I felt that many questions about who I was would never be answered unless I went back to India. Many would probably remain unanswered.

Could I track down my relatives on my father's side? Did I have cousins with whom I could establish a contact – people whose likes and dislikes and mannerisms might help explain some quirks of my own personality? How much of an Indian was I really without having been born there? Was any part of India's culture at all like the one I had experienced in Kenya?

III. THE FIRST TRIP

"For the first time in my life, I felt the comfort, the firmness of identity that name might provide, how it can carry an entire history in other people's memories, so that they might nod and say knowingly, 'Oh you are so and so's son.' No one here in Kenya would ask how to spell my name, or mangle it with an unfamiliar tongue. My name belonged and so I belonged, drawn into a web of relationships, alliances, and grudges that I did not yet understand."

Dreams from My Father by Barack Obama.

6. Rajasthan, 1992.

I ignored the prodding and tried to go back to sleep. Finally, sensing some urgency, I raised myself and looked at the watch. It was 6:00 a.m., still dark outside. We had finally got into bed at four, almost twenty-four hours after leaving Toronto. Neither Najma nor I had slept much on the plane. Irritated, I looked at Najma. Her eyes were glazed; she was sweating.

I realized her sugar levels were low. She, unfortunately, has inherited diabetes, likely from her mother.

"Do you have candies or something?" I asked.

She shook her head and could barely get the words out: "I need breakfast."

I dressed quickly and helped her to the hotel dining room where a young woman in a plain, dark sari greeted us.

She handed us over to another young woman, who escorted us to our table. A young man appeared and poured us some water. A third young woman, looking almost identical to the first two, handed us the menu.

"I know what I want – just a masala omelette, plenty of bread, two teas, and extra sugar."

"I only give out the menus, sir. Anju will take the order."

I remembered someone telling me that work in India is often divided into tasks for several people, compared to the West where we try to load up people with as much work as possible. Since labour in India is cheap, this division of labour creates employment. Each person becomes good at a specific task, guarding their territory ferociously and being careful never to inadvertently tread on another's patch. For a culture that has over four thousand castes, each with its own trade or profession and place in the Hindu hierarchy, I suppose it seems natural to mirror this model in the workplace.

Finally, Anju arrived and took the order. She wore a darker sari and had a more confident manner, identifying her as the most important link in this chain of waitresses.

We waited silently.

I was ready to yell at someone, anyone, but this would have upset Najma and made her blood sugar problems worse. Finally, I went back to the head lady and with barely disguised frustration asked her to get us tea and sugar quickly.

Najma gulped the tea loaded with sugar – something she hates – till the breakfast finally appeared.

"Sorry, sir, the cook was late," Anju apologized.

India has its own pace.

After breakfast, we sat in the hotel garden, waiting for Najma's systems to normalize.

The regal Claridges hotel was constructed in the early 1900s, when the British built a new city next to Old Delhi, the seat of the Mogul Empire, and moved the capital from Calcutta to New Delhi. Everywhere we looked there were remnants of the colonial past, with opulent rooms, majestic architecture and a decidedly British decor with printed pillows, heavy dark woods and Persian rugs.

It was a warm day, and we dozed in the comfortable lawn chairs in a semicircular garden bordered with bougainvillea and climbing roses. I imagined the *sahibs* and *memsahibs,* with long dresses and parasols, gathering here for tea parties and sundowners, served by men in turbans and tunics carrying trays laden with drinks and canapés.

****

We had flown in from Toronto two days ago, where my last business meeting had been with my boss, the president of Royal Trust. Jim was a no-nonsense, seventy-year-old, larger-than-life character with a huge potbelly – a chain smoker, who had recently been appointed to rescue the company from the verge of bankruptcy.

It was December, and I had risen at four in the morning to dig myself out of the mountains of snow that had fallen during the night. It took me an hour to get out of the driveway and I was late for the 6:30 a.m. meeting with Jim at the hotel where he lived during the weekdays. On weekends he went back to Vancouver. He'd already had his breakfast, had started smoking, and was clearly annoyed that I was late.

He wanted to make sure I could be reached in India if he needed me and directed me to meet with one of his contacts, a Dr. Raj, while I was there. The doctor ran an outsourcing company, and Jim wanted me to investigate if we could use his services to cut the cost of running my department. He had met Dr. Raj a few times and had been impressed by him.

After we'd recovered from our flight, I went to meet Dr. Raj. He was a short, stocky man who smiled a lot, shaking his head in that typically amiable but confusing Indian manner. I was given a presentation on the merits of engaging the services of his company, an earnest and long affair with many silent participants. The big advantage, they told me, was that they "fix the bugs in the software at night while you in Canada sleep peacefully, and it is there on your desk when you come next morning, Sir."

Dr. Raj then took me on a drive to Noida, a new technology park funded by the Indian government in an effort to encourage the burgeoning industry. It was choked with construction sites. I quizzed Dr. Raj about his experience in technology.

"So have you been in I.T. all these years?"

"No, no. I was section head of a very large department in ISRO, the Indian Space Research Organization."

"What section?"

"Things to do with launching" he said evasively.

"What made you leave?"

"I saw a great opportunity in the I.T. sector. Better money, better advancement. This is the future of India."

Finally, we arrived at a large, old mansion converted into offices, where I was introduced to a young programmer, Lalita. She was pretty, confident, and clearly competent as she demonstrated a variety of technologies that they thought might interest me.

Dr. Raj suddenly took over. He went into more technical detail, took a simple banking example and demonstrated the technology, dragging and dropping objects across the screen, with some showmanship.

I was impressed with how far ahead the Indian operation was, compared to what we were doing at Royal Trust and probably in most other Canadian businesses. They were not encumbered by old technology; they were starting with new technology and a new way of thinking. It seemed that introducing leading-edge technology was one area in which a developing nation was at an advantage

On our way back, he tried to impress me further.

"You saw how easily Lalita did her job. Came from a village a few years ago, very poor English but very bright girl. We can teach young people like that to be great programmers. India is becoming very advanced, you know. We are a nuclear power, we have big industries like steel, and now we will become the main supplier of software to the world, I am sure. We would like your business very much especially from Indians who settled in the West. Like you, sir. You are from Gujarat, no?"

"Yes", I said.

Just then we passed a mosque, and he grimaced.

I looked at him.

"These Muslims – always saying their prayers and producing babies."

Taken aback, I managed to hide my shock and said, "I guess that's true."

I waited tensely for him to continue.

"Filthy fanatics," he continued. "Too many in India, breeding like cockroaches. They should go where they belong – to Pakistan."

His lips curled, his eyes became cold. His sudden transformation from software guru to a hate-filled fanatic was shocking. And sickening. I put on a frozen smile. Obviously, he had not realized that I was a Muslim; he had taken me for a Hindu.

In Indian society, people generally rely on names to guess an individual's roots. A Patel is from Gujarat, a Singh from Punjab, a Das from Bengal, a Rajagopala from the South. I assume Dr.Raj had used my name, Velshi, to peg me as a Hindu from Gujarat.

How would I now tell him that I was a Muslim? I kept quiet and listened.

"I can tell you Pakistan is a mortal danger to us. But we can destroy them. We are very advanced, you know. We have the bomb and we can launch it at any time. I am blessed I had the opportunity to work on those systems, the opportunity to serve my country."

Finally, he dropped me back to the hotel and gave me his card.

What would I tell Jim when I got back?

****

That night, I put Dr. Raj out of my mind as we boarded the train that would take us through the beautifully stark province of Rajasthan. Our first tour of India was onboard the "Palace on Wheels," a luxury, moving hotel that was to take us to the capitals of the old Rajput kingdoms of Jaipur, Udaipur, Chittorgarh, Jaisalmer, Jodhpur, and Agra. Delhi station, a grand redbrick building dating from the British Imperial era, was unbearably crowded. The porters fought for clients and then jostled each other to locate their clients' compartments. The fading evening light made their task difficult and Najma helped our porters to read the names.

We flopped down into the comfortable lower bed of our sleeper compartment and watched the mad rush outside. Once the car started moving we took a brief walk through our car. It had four sleeping compartments and a small salon with a TV, tapes, newspapers, magazines, and drinks. We borrowed some of the magazines and settled into our compartment.

Two men knocked and quietly entered our compartment.

"I am Ram and this is Laxman," said the slightly taller of the two bearers who stood deferentially in front of us.

Responding to the "You've got to be kidding" look on my face, Ram added, "Truly, sir, these are our good names."

Ram and Laxman are the two main male characters of the Hindu epic *Ramayana,* Lord Rama and his brother and warrior, Laxman. It was like being introduced to a pair called Jesus and Joseph.

Our bearers, both in their early forties, were lean and about five foot eight inches, tall for Indians. They were wearing huge turbans and immaculate *sherwanis,* looked disconcertingly composed and spoke with gentle, soothing voices. Ram and Laxman were dedicated to keeping the three American couples and us in our car in absolute comfort. No request was too small or unworthy of serious attention, from taking care of laundry to getting drinks or snacks whenever we wished.

After we'd gone through Jaipur, they told us that a party had been arranged to greet the mostly international crew of travelers and all guests were requested to wear something Indian: a sari, a *kurta,* a *pashmina.*

"Laxman Ji, any ideas on what I should wear?" I asked.

Ram and Laxman both nodded, with big smiles on their faces.

"One second, sahib," Laxman said and left the compartment.

He came back with a long, coil of dark red cotton cloth covered with an unobtrusive pattern of tiny orange flowers. Then he quickly but carefully tied a turban onto my head and left a two-foot poonch, or tail, fanned out over my neck and down my back. Najma quietly watched with some amusement as the men asked me to look into the large mirror in our compartment.

I am about six feet with a moustache, but looking at my reflection in the mirror, I was surprised to see how stereotypically Indian I looked.

"You look just like a thakur," said Laxman with a wide grin on his face, and Ram nodded.

Najma burst out laughing.

A thakur, a high-caste Indian, usually a landowner, is often portrayed in Indian films as an arrogant autocrat who rides roughshod over the villagers, with his eyes always on the pretty local wenches.

****

The dress was a hit at the party. We ended up making friends with a couple from New York, Mark and Ellie, who appeared to be seasoned travellers. In the course of our conversation, Mark asked me, "What do you think of these riots?"

"Riots? What kind of riots?"

"I read in the papers today that there have been riots over some mosque that was torn down by Hindus."

"This is the first I've heard of them."

"Maybe you can find out from our bearers what's going on. I sure hope it doesn't screw up our trip."

I went looking for the holy pair and found them outside our quarters. They were furtively fiddling with the reservation card placed on the door of our compartment.

"What are you doing?"

They stayed silent like two schoolboys caught in the act of mischief.

"Nothing, sahib. Just adjusting your card," Ram mumbled at last.

"Something wrong with it?"

"No, sahib."

"But you changed it?"

They looked at each other.

"We were just correcting it."

"What was the correction?" I said and pulled the card out.

I realized our names had been shortened to Mr. and Mrs. Velshi. Our first names had been removed.

"Why are our first names no longer there?"

"It's better, sir. Safer."

"Safer?" I asked.

"Yes, with all this going on, it's better that people don't see that your first names are Mehboob and Najma."

"What's wrong with the names?" I said, starting to get irritated.

"Sir, they are Muslim."

"Yes, and is that bad?"

"Did you read about what happened in Ayodhya?"

"I don't know what you're talking about."

"Wait one minute, Sahib." Laxman scurried away and came back with a newspaper.

"Babri Masjid destroyed!" the headline read.

Two days earlier, L.K. Advani, a leader in the Hindu BJP (Bharatya Janata Party), had ridden a *rath* (a chariot) into the grounds of the Babri mosque, in the holy city of Ayodhya. Hindu nationalists have long claimed that five hundred years ago, Mir Baki, the commander-in-chief of the first Mogul emperor Babur, had destroyed a Hindu temple built on Ram Janmabhoomi, a site believed to be the birthplace of Lord Rama to erect the mosque in honour of the emperor. Advani's spectacular "repossession" of the Hindu holy ground had whipped Hindu mobs into frenzy, and they had razed the mosque to the ground.

"What does this have to do with us?" I asked after scanning the article.

"Sa'ab, after this tragedy, the Muslims got very angry and attacked some Hindus. Now Hindus are killing Muslims."

"Here? in Rajasthan?"

"Yes, Sa'ab. We don't expect any problems on the train. You are all tourists but it is better to be safe, just in case something happens. You are travelling with gora log–

you are safe, they never attack white people. They'll know you are foreigners and won't touch you, but just to be sure, sir, let's not show your names. We don't want anything to happen to you."

Najma, as usual, was sanguine.

"If there's a problem, we look so Indian – and if we call ourselves by our surnames, how will anyone know? I don't think we need to worry."

As I drifted off, I recalled the Indian classic *A Train to Pakistan* by Khushwant Singh, about tensions between Sikhs and Muslims that erupt into mayhem when a trainful of murdered Sikhs arrives into their little town. Set during the Partition, it's a fictional tale based on real tragic events, when fury and madness gripped Hindus, Muslims and Sikhs, leading them to brutally mass murder and rape those they had lived with in peace for centuries, often as friends and neighbours.

I fell into a bizarre dream.

The train stops and I get out to investigate. Dr Raj, shouting orders in Swahili, is leading a mob of dhoti-wearing, sword-wielding Indians and dreadlocked black Mau Mau warriors, armed with machetes, carrying out a search of the train. The shouting, pleas for mercy, and orders become louder as the mob approaches our compartment. I lock up our door but soon someone starts pounding on the door. Dr. Raj is screaming that I am a Muslim pretending to be a Hindu. Someone finally breaks the door down and an Indian orders two Mau Mau to take off my pajamas.

When they see that I am circumcised, proof that I am a Muslim, he lifts a machete..

I wake up from the dream, drenched in sweat. My first thought is that we should cut our trip short and I look at Najma, sleeping peacefully, snoring gently. I breathe deeply and try to relax.

****

I can still recall my own circumcision.

I was seven when my aunts sat my mother down and gave her some advice. They told her that my upbringing as a Hindu was going to leave me nowhere, without an identity. "This child can't make up his mind whether he is a Sikh or Hindu or whatever. You have to make an Ismaili out of him or he will grow up confused, marry outside the community and only Allah knows what else."

Here I was, a bundle of various Indian languages and identities, about to be rechristened, as it were, and renamed Mehboob. I preferred Manu and changed it to simply Mike several years later.

But my aunts had a particular and painful metamorphosis in mind; I was to be circumcised. I vividly remember the agony and the trauma of being held down and losing consciousness within seconds. There was no anesthesia. I still redden at the pain and embarrassment of it all.

Nanima invited all my aunts and cousins to my coming-out party as a newly minted Muslim. She made me sit next to her, to protect me from the jibes of my sniggering cousins, who were having a field day. I remember nanima admonishing my mother just before the party started: "Dolu, you've always been a *budhu*. Why would you not get the boy circumcised at birth? Had you decided to bring him up as a Hindu? Look at him. He can't even stand up. He's in agony. Now that this piece of skin is off, are you going to bring him up as a Muslim?"

Tradition required that money be given to the child or the mother at the time of the circumcision. Nanima started the ball rolling by giving me a hundred shillings, an unheard-of amount of money. In the end, I received almost enough money to fulfill my long-held boyhood dream of buying my own bicycle,. I remember wondering if it was worth the agony I had to go through.

****

Two days after we heard the news about the riots, a curfew was imposed on Rajasthan and Gujarat.

This was to be my third experience of a curfew. The first, in Nairobi during the Mau Mau War, was imposed when I had just learned to read the papers. I remember pictures of ferocious black men with dreadlocks, sometimes covered in cheetah skin, accused of slaughtering white farmer families in gruesome ways. These accounts of horrible murder stood in sharp contrast to daily life in Nairobi. The days were sunny, the air subdued, and the evenings menacing, but other than reports of occasional shots at night, life carried on normally. The newspapers were the biggest source of fear. It was much later that I discovered that much bloodshed was going on outside Nairobi in carefully concealed detention camps, where the British were carrying out torture, medical experiments, and mass killing of the Kikuyu. By now it has passed into the realm of history and few care to remember apart from a handful of elderly survivors of the horrors.

My second brush with a curfew was in Kampala when I was at Makerere University. The prime minister at the time, Milton Obote, ordered the arrest of the President of Uganda, Frederick Mutesa – the kabaka, or king, of the Buganda people. General Idi Amin, then commander of the army, surrounded the royal palace one evening in a bid to capture the king. President Mutesa managed to escape before Amin's troops could enter his palace, but some of his wives, children, and attendants were brutally murdered in the sacking and burning of the palace that followed. A curfew was declared but life on the campus went on as before. Nothing much was reported in the media except the escape of the president. My friends, students at Mulago, the teaching hospital, told me of hundreds of bodies of the Buganda people being brought in during the night and stacked in the mortuary like sacks of sugar. The corpses showed signs of torture and rape, most likely by Amin's ruthless troops.

And now if the past was anything to go by, I was going to have a surrealistic existence for the next few weeks with normalcy during the day and killings of the 'enemy tribe' during the night. The press was not going to tell the whole truth and our lives as Muslims could be in danger. Whenever I read reports of riots in the papers I wondered what was really happening and was not being reported.

I forced myself to focus on our trip. The bare, arid land of Rajasthan was dotted with the historic cities of Jodhpur, Jaisalmer, Udaipur, and Chittorgarh. The sands changed from light colours in the mornings to an almost blazing red at sunset, the formation of dunes gave way to rocky hills and dry gulches strewn with cacti and clumps of thick grass. Near small towns and villages, the children came out and waved at us merrily.

Each major city had legends surrounding its rulers, princes who fought heroic wars against the Muslim invaders and whose women committed mass *sutee,* preferring to be burned alive than captured by the enemy.

Every morning, after a hearty breakfast served in our private salon, we set forth on a day tour of a different city. At some of the stations, we were garlanded before we began our routine visit of the temples, forts, palaces, and museums, followed by lunch at a palace hotel. In every city there was a palace, built by a Rajput prince of a bygone era that had been converted into a hotel. Sometimes the surviving princes were pointed out to us, usually sitting quietly in their gardens, next to their wing of the palace. I had imagined the maharajas to be tall, erect, moustachoed specimens of manhood in princely garb, not the short, inconspicuous men with slight paunches, dressed in plain shirts and pants.

After lunch, we would spend a couple of hours shopping, usually in the old part of the city. *Dhandha* – commerce – was carried on with offers, counteroffers, handshakes, and sealed with cups of tea. Promptly at four, we would be bussed out of the business area. Twice, when someone was late getting back to the bus, we were whisked away amid the sound of gunfire and the sight of people running for cover. It was as if at four, the Indians, famous for not observing time, would promptly close up shop and automatically resume fighting.

I wondered what these gentle shopkeepers, beggars, and labourers – who joked, pleaded, and bargained with us – actually did after rushing to close up their businesses for the day. Did they hide at home? Take up arms? Join the marauding gangs of murderers, rapists, and arsonists?

Every night we had pre-dinner drinks back on the train, followed by a seven-course dinner, a brandy and a smoke. Nobody wanted to discuss the riots and people were generally in a holiday mood. There was nothing to do but enjoy the trip.

The highlight of the trip, as expected, proved to be the Taj Mahal at sunset. As we slowly walked towards the famous mausoleum, the marble seemed to come alive, changing its colours from white to suggestions of blue and red. The coolness inside the building, the stonework, the gaping wounds left by the ripping out of the precious stones by colonizers, paid silent testimony to the marvel of engineering and its survival over five hundred years. There were no images of Mumtaz Mahal, the empress in whose memory the Emperor Shah Jehan had built the mausoleum but her presence pervaded the mausoleum. I wondered what kind of a woman had inspired one of the wonders of the world, a woman who has become the symbol of love for every Indian regardless of his or her religion. Mumtaz Mahal had died during the birth of their 14th child.

We still remember this luxury trip – sumptuous and elegant. We were treated like the royalty whose palaces we had come to see. But more than that, I remember the surrealism of the situation: the killing and rampaging we knew was going on at night as we slept in our berths, the train chugging on impassively through the violent darkness.

****

Back in Delhi, there was no sign of the rioting – only complaints from tourists and shopkeepers about the unrelenting traffic and pollution. The politicians and civil servants appeared to be carrying on oblivious to the turmoil. We took tuk-tuks to go shopping at Connaught Place. The streets and shops were full of people, and we wandered around enjoying the warm weather. Everything seemed normal, nobody was concerned, and the papers were nonchalantly reporting sporadic attacks. I found the coexistence of normality, the festiveness of December holidays and the insanity of the religious riots going on throughout the country unnerving. Why wasn't someone appealing for these attacks to stop, why weren't the army or police being called in?

I was anxious to return to Toronto but Najma persuaded me that we should take advantage of the Indian Airlines passes we had purchased. They allowed us to fly anywhere in India for the next three weeks. I reluctantly agreed and we started to plan a trip.

We spread the map of India on our bed and debated where to go. There were so many places still to visit: Cochin, Goa, Chennai, and the hill stations. Finally we decided to spend a few days on the legendary beaches near Trivandrum at the southern tip of India and then fly to Calcutta and perhaps take in some shows. Calcutta held a fascination for both of us as the cultural Mecca of India, a place where great artists such as Tagore and the filmmaker Satyajit Ray had lived and created their works. Our final destination was going to be Mumbai from where we'd fly back to Toronto.

I picked up the phone beside my bed and called Ramesh, our travel agent. Ramesh a well-built, dark man with oiled straight hair, and a thick moustache, was a great salesman full of convincing arguments.

The phone rang twice and was picked up on the third ring: "Good morning, sir. How can I help you?"

"Good morning, Ramesh, this is Mr. Velshi. I want to use my Indian Airlines pass to travel to a couple of places," I said

"Haven't you heard sir? The Indian Airlines have decided to go on strike. Why these people keep doing this is beyond me. Sir, we need airline deregulation in this country,"

"So I can't fly anywhere?"

"No sir, you can take train. We have the best railway system in the world, sir."

"Maybe we can just change our tickets and go back earlier to Canada, perhaps directly from Delhi."

"But why go back early, sir? You are worried about these *chotee batae*? Such small matters mean nothing in India. I can tell you stories of what happened to my family during the Partition that would fill your eyes with tears. Also sir, going back early is very difficult. All the flights are booked. Also you are booked to fly from Mumbai. If you could manage to change that to Delhi, it would be very expensive.

"How can I get to Mumbai?"

"On the train, overnight on the Rajdhani. Best service in India, sir."

"Tickets are available?"

"Of course, I can arrange, sir. Our agency has many connections, sir."

"Should we take first class or second?" Perhaps a silly question to ask.

"Whatever your pleasure is, sir. But I recommend first class."

"Ok. Can you get tickets for the day after tomorrow?"

"It is possible."

"How much for the two of us?"

"There will be an extra charge for service at such short notice, unfortunately."

"Why?" I pretend to be naïve.

"Well, the booking clerk is a friend, and he will make a special effort on your behalf, but these people are so underpaid, sir. A few dollars means a lot towards savings for his daughter's dowry. A thousand rupees for you and a thousand for Madam."

"All right. Go ahead."

We decided to explore Old Delhi the next day. We rented a tuk-tuk and asked to be taken to the Jamia Mosque, the largest and most famous mosque in India, the Jamia Masjid. Tanks, jeeps, police officers, and tough jawans of the Indian army surrounded it and we were stopped from entering the mosque.

A young army officer walked up and said, "No entry, sir, please move on."

He turned around abruptly and we stood a little shocked and gazed for few moments at the mosque before moving. We began to stroll through the narrow streets of the Old City, a Dickensian neighbourhood that has become a predominantly Muslim quarter. The streets were tense and armed soldiers stood at every corner. If this massive presence was designed to prevent *"chotee batae,"* I wondered what firepower would be needed to prevent a major upheaval.

The shops and stalls of the market were filled with bearded men, women in hijab and a few tourists. The air was subdued; the shopping was done quickly, purposefully without the usual bargaining. The restaurants that served barbecued meat, biriyanis and goat feet curry looked empty and uninviting. Uncomfortable, we grabbed a cold coconut water and a samosa each and headed back to the livelier, unconcerned Connaught Place in New Delhi.

The next day, we took the Rajdhani overnight to Mumbai.

7. Mumbai, 1992-93.

Upon arrival in Mumbai, I persuaded Najma to stay at the legendary Taj Hotel by the Gateway of India in Colaba, the tourist and financial district of the city. She objects to staying in expensive hotels but agreed that it would be a safer place and reluctantly agreed to my little subterfuge to get a large discount.

Ramesh had coached me in how to act like a local: "Don't show your passports, tell them you live in Delhi, use my address as your own. After all we are like family now. Always speak in Hindi – you speak very good Hindi, sir. If you speak good English, they'll know you're a foreigner and you will be robbed, sir. They pay twice the tariff that the locals have to. And the Taj is a safe place, just in case there is a problem."

The first evening, Najma suggested we go to the mosque in Colaba.

"Yes, sounds great. I'd like to," I replied.

"You sound enthusiastic," Najma said suspiciously.

We walked from the hotel by the sea to the khanne, which was about fifteen minutes away, through the Colaba market. It was chocked with small shops, stalls on the sidewalk and touts urging us to come into the shops, asking us if we were from England, or America, anything to engage us in conversation and get us to look at their wares. Colaba had little space to walk but it offered laughter, surprise, colours and smells from its fruit stalls, mithai shops full of colourful Indian sweetmeats, shoe and clothing stores, and all manner of unusual shops.

The mosque was nondescript, a simple hall with a plain entrance. The service was quick and efficient. When it was over I sidled to the front of the *nandi paath* where the food offerings were stacked up, ready for the auction. When a chicken *akni* – rice pilaf with chicken and an onion, vinegar, and cucumber salad on the side – came up, I began to bid against a large, bald man with a thick neck who was standing close to me. He finally stopped bidding when he saw I was determined to take that *akni*. He was in the green uniform of a volunteer, adorned with a badge that simply said 'lieutenant' and medals carrying white, red and blue ribbon. He must have done *seva* for years. Najma's mother had made lieutenant after decades of service and had worn a smart frock of the same colour.

The lieutenant turned to me and said, "My name is Sadroo. *Baharna cho?*"

"Yes, I'm a newcomer – from Canada. My name is Mehboob."

"Where are you staying?"

"At a hotel nearby."

"Which one?" he persisted.

"The Taj," I sheepishly confessed.

He looked at me disapprovingly.

"Why pay so much money, *bhai?* I can give you names of hotels owned by Ismailis, much cheaper and safer. You give *bijness* to a brother and none of this drinking and partying. There will be prayers twice a day."

"God help me," I thought and decided to lie," Sounds good, but I have already paid in advance."

A little concerned, I added, "Surely the Taj is a safe place?"

"Probably, but too much *dekhawa*. Better not to make a show and live in a place nobody notices. You know what the Maula says, 'Never make too much show.' Besides, you know of this *locho* going on between Hindus and Muslims. We are registering all Ismailis just in case it hits Mumbai."

"And then what?"

"We have safe houses, food, security. You know, a little something for the police to make sure nothing happens to us. We've made every arrangement, you know," he said, sounding important and confidential.

"I was thinking of going to Gujarat, to look for my relatives. You think it's worth trying?" I asked.

He looked at me with exaggerated disbelief.

"Arrey, Na, na. Why put your head in the mouth of death? Stay away. We've already lost three Ismaili lives. Even here we are telling our women to dress simply, remove all jewellery, don't do anything to draw attention. Next week no one will be bringing *nandi* plates to *khanne*. Things can get bad *bhai,* trust me. I suggest you register

and we will come and get you or phone you if it's safe to take a taxi."

I registered.

After he finished taking down all the details, he leaned over and said, "You know, the less said about this registration outside the mosque, the better."

I remembered nanima's words of warning: "Never tell anyone, especially other Muslims, anything about what goes on in the *khanne.*" I thought she was going a little gaga in her old age. As a young boy, whenever I went to the mosque, I would hear firmans emphasizing the virtues of education and frugality. The young should get a university education, we were going to enter the world of meritocracy. The brightest would get the best jobs, regardless of connections and colour. Weddings were a time for celebration, not an opportunity to show off the parents' wealth, funerals should be simple: no coffins or headstones (no point showing off your wealth when you were six feet under). The general message was to stay low key. But I always wondered why Nanima seemed to think these were state secrets of some sort. They weren't really that spectacular. In fact, if I divulged them to my friends or family, I was quite sure I'd be met with a big yawn.

The Ismailis, like most minorities, suffer from paranoia and have dealt with their long history of persecution by becoming markedly private and low key. As Sadroo said, the philosophy has always been one of no *dekhawa* – no ostentation. But living in their own colonies, emphasizing education, particularly the education of girls, and allowing women freedom of dress singles Ismailis out, certainly in the Muslim world. Though Ismailis no longer build colonies and schools exclusively for themselves, they still grapple with the conundrum of being progressive but wanting to remain inconspicuous.

In the warm moonlit night outside the mosque, people appeared so relaxed and friendly, that I couldn't help feeling that Sadroo was being alarmist. We returned to our spacious hotel room with its high ceiling and large patio doors that led to a small balcony. We sat down on the balcony overlooking the glimmering Arabian Sea and ate the delicious akni. The brilliantly lit Gateway of India a hundred yards or so south of us, its grounds full of milling crowds and to the north, two miles or so away was Chowpatty beach, the strip where my father and his sister had walked many decades ago. It had taken him weeks to cross the ocean and now a five-hour flight can take me to Nairobi any day of the week.

****

The next evening we explored Colaba and did some shopping, taking refuge in the cool shops away from the pesky stall owners. We noticed a number of Ismaili shops, mostly in the shoe business and a peek inside revealed most had a picture of the Aga Khan, adorning one of the walls.

Najma needed shoes, and after expending much energy in comparison-shopping, she chose Mumbai Best Shoes.

"Ya Ali Madat," we said to the owner.

He smiled and replied, *"Maula Ali Madat."*

He slipped into Gujarati and asked, "Where are you from?"

"Canada."

"We get a lot of Canadians. Let me show what is popular with them."

As the shopkeeper and Najma chatted and meandered through the women's section, I was again struck by the power of this simple greeting and presence of a picture of the Imam to establish an instant connection, an Ismaili identity that binds the many languages and racial groups.

While he showed Najma what Canadians like, I sat down and enjoyed the cup of tea that had magically appeared. I'd heard that many shoe shop owners had belonged to the caste of *chamars* – leatherworkers – one of the lowest Hindu castes, before they had been converted to Ismailism generations ago. They had moved from villages that ignored and even despised them to big metropolises and become very successful. Theirs would be quite a story to write.

Najma picked three pairs and got a special 'Ismaili' discount as well as a volume discount. They were delicate looking pretty sandals, unfit for Canadian weather, and I assumed were for wearing in the mosque.

We wandered out into the sun-baked street to look for a snack and a cold drink and after dodging cars, tuk tuks and the touts, we stumbled upon Leopold's. From the outside there was nothing especially noteworthy about its long glass front. Inside was a two-storied, high-ceilinged café, full of mirrors and dark wood paneling with marble topped tables set so close together you could hardly walk between them. The menu, a curious blend and mix of Indian and European food, was long and comprehensive.

Leopold's immediately took us back to another time and place – to Friends Corner in Nairobi in the early seventies-a restaurant where Najma and I would go for a late night coffee. It had the same sort of menu, ambience and mixed clientele of young locals and overseas tourists. Friends Corner is gone but Leopold's has now achieved legendary status.

What Najma and I naïvely thought of as a little discovery of our own, has quite a history. Opened in 1871 by an Iranian family and apparently named after the late Belgian king, it's still owned by Iranians: Farhang and Ferzad Jehani. Gregory Roberts, an escaped Australian convict, went on to make Leopold's world famous with his book *Shantaram,* an account of how he established contact with the Mumbai underworld and it is in his footsteps that many European tourists pay a visit to Leopold's.

For the next ten days, we spent at least an hour at Leopold's every morning, having breakfast, usually a masala omelette, while reading the *Times of India*. We followed the story of the "communal riots," as the reciprocal murderous attacks by Hindus and Muslims were referred to in the papers. Sometimes we dropped in during the evenings for a beer and chips, sitting near the doorway so we could watch the crowds, our popular pastime in India. The street vendors were pleading with tourists and skillfully drawing in young Americans and Europeans with backpacks; the local businessmen deftly avoided the mêlée; old men and housewives haggled with the fruit and vegetable vendors and a newcomer, looking unsure, was being teased and given lessons in street trading.

Leopold's is now a special place for Najma and I, a bridge between memories of our living in Nairobi and Mumbai.

****

On the night of January 2, 1993 we took a cab to the airport.

We noticed smoke covering the road, as we got closer to our destination. I peered closely into the darkness and saw that it was pouring out of a string of burning tires. I could see that all the shops in Mahim, near the airport, were barricaded.

"What's going on?" I asked the driver.

"Just a Hindu Mussalman *tanta,* nothing to worry about. No one will stop a taxi. Where are you from?"

"From Canada," we replied guardedly, "Gujaratis."

"Hindus?"

A white lie – a muted yes.

"Nothing to worry then."

A courtly old waiter at the Taj had imparted wisdom that came to mind, "Sir, no need to give your Muslim name, especially these days, when someone asks. You were a Hindu once."

We spent the rest of the terrifying drive in silence. There was an eerie quiet, darkness punctuated by flickering fires, small gangs of men running across the road and the driver, for all his bravado, looked scared. I rehearsed what I would say if we were stopped. With the best of my English Canadian accent, I would state that we were Canadians on our way to the airport. If they spoke an

Indian language, I would reply in broken Hindi. Should I flash our passports and take the chance they would not demand to see our names? It was unlikely they would attack foreigners.

We grabbed each other's hands in relief as the entrance of the airport came into view. As soon as I took my seat on the plane, I ordered a large scotch.

****

We landed in London in the early hours of the next day, and Mukesh, Najma's brother-in-law, picked us up. He's a Hindu as it happens. Najma had brought some presents for her sister Nilu and their two boys and we were looking forward to spending the day with their family before going back to Toronto.

It was a cool, slightly foggy London morning and Mukesh asked many questions about our trip as he drove towards his home. The house was a spacious detached two-storey property in a suburb of North London. The garden looked surprisingly green. The curtains were drawn; the house felt dark and empty as Mukesh invited us into the kitchen to sit at a small table.

"The boys are sleeping in and Nilu is on her way to Mombasa, " Mukesh said, catching us by surprise " I wanted you to be sitting at home, not standing in an airport when we talk about what's happened."

"One of my parents?" Najma asked in a trembling voice.

" Your father passed away last night."

Najma's eyes watered but she stayed silent for what seemed an eternity. In her jeans and sweater she looked travel weary and suddenly small.

Finally, she asked, "How did he die?"

"He was sitting outside in the sun, enjoying his coffee at a little Arab café and smoking a cigarillo, and he just dropped off."

A look of relief, almost thankfulness appeared on her face and she said, "I'm glad. It's a good way to go. How is my mother?"

"She said the same thing as you just did—he was lucky to have died peacefully, sitting with his friends."

Najma sat quietly for a few minutes and after visiting the washroom, came back; her face washed and insisting on making breakfast for all of us.

We had some tea and toast and chatted a bit about Najma's father, the colourful, temperamental man with a love of food, music, and travel. She recalled how he'd often taken her to ride on the ferris wheel owned by his Bhadala friends – the men who operated tours of Mombasa harbour in their little boats and ran booths and rides at many festivals. His other friends were ship's staff on passenger liners to India, cruise ships from Europe and America, British Navy vessels, and *dhows* from Arabian countries like Oman and Yemen that gave Mombasa its vibrant nautical life. She still remembered the names of some of those boats – the *Sakura Maru*, the *Amsterdam, SS Karanja* and it was those tales of sea adventures that got into her soul and gave her the wanderlust.

She remembered working for her pocket money and receiving four shillings for working on two hundred bills of lading- enough money for a movie and a piece of roasted spicy cassava.

****

After breakfast, Najma went to sleep and I started to read the newspapers, accounts of horrific events in Mumbai. On the day we'd flown out, a number of men suspected of being Muslims were stopped by Hindu mobs. Some of the circumcised men were executed on the sidewalks right outside the Taj Hotel. I remember thinking to myself – this is 1993, how can we be murdering people for practicing a different faith? Some of them, like me, could have been secular Muslims.

The second of January became an anniversary on which Najma would offer the customary food and prayers at the mosque in memory of her father. For me, it is also a reminder of the day we left Mumbai, the start of the massacre that followed.

As soon as we got back to Canada, I was drawn into the middle of a storm at work. My company, Royal Trust, had been declared insolvent and was in the process of being sold. A hundred-and-fifty-year-old company had been driven into the ground by terrible credit decisions and an orgy of wild lending. The CEO had been let go.

As the head of IT, I was part of a team that had to make detailed presentations of the company's technology, systems, and budgets to several potential buyers – mostly large banks interested in taking over the company. I suspect some members of the teams that came shopping were there to get a look at the books, the systems, the future plans, and the inner workings of a once great company gone bankrupt. Looking for a buyer, under the scrutiny of the government and the competitors, was an awful, humiliating experience.

For me the stress of the takeover was complicated by another consideration. My key staff was out searching for jobs, and I spent hours trying to retain them while negotiating with management for staying bonuses until the takeover was completed.

On a personal level, I faced the threat of a financial meltdown. Having become an executive, like many others, I had been 'encouraged' (more or less forced) to borrow money to purchase company shares over the previous five years and now owed the company far more than the value of my house and other assets put together. It had seemed a risk worth taking and we had never imagined that a large financial Canadian institution like Royal Trust would be put on the auction block.

Every evening, Najma and I went out for a long walk, no matter how cold it was, to work off the daily stress of worrying about the loss of my job and everything we owned. It was reminiscent of the time when I had failed my final year, worked twelve hours a day, run every night, and tried to beat insomnia. But now I had Najma to share my burden and the children to play with.

On weekends, I continued to read the *Times of India,* feeling somehow compelled to follow events in Mumbai. In the weeks after we left, gangs of Hindu thugs had attacked predominantly Muslim neighbourhoods using a list of addresses where Muslims were living. The Shiv Sena, the army of Lord Shiva, and the government of Maharashtra State were considered the main collaborators in the killings. The less organized Muslim minority retaliated, and in three months almost a thousand people were killed, two-thirds of them Muslims.

Eventually a group of people seeking revenge, led by Muslim gangsters, organized themselves into a squad that carried out a single massive retaliatory attack against the authorities who had stood back and not protected them.

On the afternoon of March 9, within a two-hour period, thirteen bombs exploded in downtown Mumbai. The targets included the Mumbai stock exchange, the Air India building, the Shiv Sena Bhavan , major theatres and hotels. Two hundred and fifty civilians were killed, with many more seriously injured.

The Indian government launched investigations against senior members of the Shiv Sena, and the Muslim gang leaders. The Shiv Sena, Army of the Lord Shiva, is an extremist Hindu party then led by Bal Thackeray, a self-confessed admirer of Hitler, who particularly hated Muslims. The party has great political power and has had a hand in running the government of the State of Maharashtra and the city of Mumbai to this day.

The gangsters fled the country and it soon became apparent that the top leaders of the Shiv Sena were simply too powerful to be prosecuted effectively. Their cases became tied up in web of Indian politics and the notoriously slow pace of Indian courts.

The India of my mother's Geeta and Gandhi's promises had, in one short trip, turned out to be anything but gentle. I lost interest.

****

The turmoil in my own life finally settled as Royal Trust was taken over and I became part of the huge Royal bank, with its own politics and bureaucracy. I faced the challenge of learning to live in an institution that resembled an army. There were battalions of clerks, who reported to managers, who informed vice-presidents, who summarized for senior vice-presidents, and at the very top of the ladder sat the commander, the CEO, who was paid an astronomical salary to make sense of what was reported to him and oversee the daily flows of billions of dollars. An old boys club, almost exclusively older white men, ran the bank. They lived in the city's choice neighbourhoods, Rosedale and Mississauga; had cottages in Muskoka or places with other magical-sounding names; and were godfathers to each other's children. I felt uncomfortable at the cocktail parties. I realized that it was at these little gatherings and on golf courses that the major actions were initiated and crucial information was exchanged. A few discreet words in the right ear made things happen, things that it would take an outsider months, if ever, to set in motion.

As an outsider myself, I had to establish credibility and gain the respect of this elite tribe. Some diehards did not believe that someone like me could run a large department and chose to deal with some of my subordinates they had known for a long time. There were polite and deadly turf wars between major departments that took up a lot of energy to deal with.

In my department there existed another tribe, the older technologists and original architects of the company's systems, who I had to deal with on a day-to-day basis. The most senior of these, whom I called Foxy Phil, had hired many of the employees from the U.K. He not only opposed me at every step but also more generally the introduction of banking on the Internet (not a robust infrastructure, he intoned), the use of Indian outsourcing (unreliable) and various other initiatives.

But there were younger, more progressive people who helped me to bring in new technologies and ideas. That was the exciting part of the job. I travelled often with major suppliers to the research labs in the US and Europe and conferences where major new ideas and technologies were being discussed and developed.

I was fortunate to report to Ken, the head of my department, who respected me and was supportive of my career at the bank. He was the third person in my career to give me a major promotion. The other two David and Paul were senior executives in my previous jobs who appreciated my work and greatly supported me. I owe a great deal to these men.

I became the first non-white senior vice-president of the bank and with it inherited many perks, a large corner office and staff to help me. The promotion gained me respect within the Ismaili community, as well as in other institutions who wanted me to speak at their functions and get involved in other leadership roles. I was naturally pleased with my success but somehow I did not consider it to be as great an achievement as some others did. The evenings started to get filled with cocktail parties and receptions and ate into my time with Abid and Sameena.

The bank was the most professional, well-organized place I have worked for and though those who supported me suggested that I claw my way up to executive vice-president or even vice-chairman, I decided to exit at the earliest possible opportunity, hopefully with a little nest egg. I already had ulcers and high-blood pressure, and above all I wanted to spend time with the children who were growing up quickly.

Najma and I dreamed of paying off the mortgage, getting the children off to university and fulfilling our dream of travelling.

It was six years after I left the bank that Abid dropped his little bombshell about getting a job in India. My first reaction was fear, but then Najma reasoned that over a hundred and fifty million Muslims lived in India, and things were now settled. Let him go.

IV. TRAVELS WITH ABID

" Mumbai has the best skill pool in India, it pays the best salaries, but sometimes the best is not good enough. It is not good enough because we believe that in Mumbai straw can turn to gold and that Rumpelstiltskin isn't a fairy tale figure but Dhirubhai Ambani himself who turned himself from a petrol-pump attendant into a petrochemical magnate. Everyone wants to get there, yesterday."

The Cult of the Golden Bull by Nina Martyris.

8. A high tech job in India, 2005.

Abid phoned us every week often while he was walking around Colaba Market in Mumbai.

It was seventy years earlier that my father and his sister had gone for their stroll along the seafront – not far from that very market. It had taken my father weeks to get to Kenya and then many lonely months of working as a warehouse boy learning to do bookkeeping. Abid had left home but communications technology kept us in constant and close touch whereas my father began a new life, severing all ties with the past.

Within hours of arriving in Mumbai, Abid had bought a chip for his phone so it could operate in India. With mobile rates in India amongst the cheapest in the world, we had a comfortable lengthy chat. Najma and I directed him to Leopold's and suggested dishes he might like.

A week later, he e-mailed.

"Where do I start? Mumbai is probably the most hectic, overpopulated city I have ever been to. I feel overwhelmed with the sights, sounds and smells. Mumbai is full of traffic all the time . . . sometimes there are traffic jams at 12:00 at night . . . it's just insane. The pollution here is just ridiculous. Its just mind blowing how the city, constantly in a state of chaos, works. You don't know what overcrowding is until you walk into Mumbai.
But for every negative to this hectic city there are at least a couple of good things. Generally people are friendly and respectful, unless they are trying to sell you something in which case they are most likely trying to rip you off. I wish I had learned an Indian language. I love the food here and it's absolutely safe to walk around. Whenever I am a bit homesick – which is rare because I am so busy – I can eat something at Leopold's that reminds me of mom's cooking."

We became worried when we read in the papers that Mumbai was experiencing one of its worst monsoon seasons, and immediately called him to ask if he'd bought an umbrella.

He burst out laughing.

"Sheets of rain are falling, Dad. In one day one metre of rain, the worst in the history of Mumbai. I walked with water well above my knees. I bought an umbrella, but it blew away."

So we suffered through the occupational hazard of being parents- helpless worrying. After two weeks he was sent to a centre near Trivandrum, Kerala at the southern tip of India for training and eventually found time to call and chat.

"Where exactly are you?" I asked.

"This is where the three oceans meet – the Arabian Sea, the Bay of Bengal, and the Indian Ocean. You can watch the sun set and the moon rise together; the palms and the sound of the surf just make it stunning, so different from Mumbai. Anyway, we are in classes ten hours a day."

"What are they teaching?"

"It's all about company technology, standards and practices, and so on – pretty good stuff. But then they teach presentation skills and role-playing. That's hilarious. And there are differences between the city guys and the 'villagers.'"

"In what way?"

"The city slickers from the big cities like Mumbai and Delhi are confident and well dressed, and they speak reasonable Hinglish(Hindi accented English). The 'villagers' are shy and mumble whilst the city guys make fun of the poor guys. And of course there are plenty of foreigners like me – from Turkey, Brazil, all over the world."

"What about the food?"

" It's all cafeteria based. It all reminds me of elementary school. You have a recess, and at lunchtime you line up for food. And they stare at you if you talk to the girls."

"I guess it's conservative."

"The girls actually blush if you talk to them."

"And the food?"

"The food is great. I like *idli*, *sambar* and all those South Indian vegetarian dishes, but I have to get a good North Indian chicken curry soon. I never realized that the northerners and southerners are quite different people with different languages and food, and they look different. The Southerners seem more educated . . . lots of M.Sc.s and even Ph.Ds."

After completing his training, Abid was recruited as an analyst with a unit serving the central government in Delhi. His biggest challenge turned out to be finding a decent place to live in the city. He managed to find a tiny room downtown, but the noise and the smells made sleep impossible. "I have decided to spend a considerable amount more, in Indian terms, to find a livable place," he wrote.

I offered to help out because I considered his internship to be part of his education, but he refused adamantly and quickly located a place in Hauz Khas, a small artists' colony in a corner of New Delhi. The commute was long, he had to work ten or eleven hours a day, as do most Indians, and the dogs chased him at night when he came in at ten. For weeks he sounded tired and depressed but finally he found a roommate to share an apartment closer to the downtown.

"So who's the roomie?"

"Ah . . . someone called Malti."

"So it's an Indian girl?"

"Well, I am in India."

"Her parents approve?"

"Are you kidding? They don't even know. I can't pick up the phone just in case they are calling. They would have a bird."

"So you like her?"

"Dad, she'd just a roomie. A friend."

****

At work, Abid was excited to meet brilliant and dedicated civil servants, but after a few months, he realized that they were hopelessly tied up with red tape and it took complex machinations at the higher levels to inch things along even a little.

He looked for another posting and soon moved to Mumbai as a software engineer, into a job that he felt was beneficial for his future. He was impressed at the amount of software some young programmers could produce in a few hours – an amount, he said, that would take an average Canadian programmer a week to turn out.

But there were problems.

"Work, for anyone who is interested, is crazy," he wrote in one e-mail. "People here work some serious hours. Start time is usually 9 a.m. After leaving at 7:30 p.m., feeling like I have put in as much as I can, there are still tons of people working on . . . Saturdays is half day, till 4 p.m. One of the people I work with stays till 10:00 almost every night . . . he is great at his job but he's a machine! I think I am going to have a pretty intense few months here . . .but it's probably good for me . . . reality has finally set in."

And then there was the strict hierarchy: seniority counted, and elders had to be respected and listened to – lessons taught in Indian homes. The programmers waited patiently to be told what to do next and never disagreed with the boss even if he was blatantly wrong.

Most requests were doubly affirmed: "Yes, yes, we can do it." Indians find it impossible to say "No" even to things that are just obviously unreasonable and impractical. The most negative answer is "Let's see. I will try."

Jobs were so precious that no one was prepared to appear to be the least bit obstructive.

Abid resented the fact that not only had work become such a major part of his life, but also he had no say in running the projects to which he was assigned.

Frustrated, he sat through meetings where the hierarchy was so strict that no one spoke out of turn. There was little innovation and too much kowtowing.

His social life was an equally steep learning curve.

The get-togethers of the sexes consisted of going to Bollywood films followed by sharing pizzas and often a 'music party' at someone's flat, where someone with a good voice would sing and the rest would join in. While they all knew the lyrics he had no idea what they were singing.

Eventually, his social contact with his co-workers became limited to two young men he admired immensely. Jagdish, a young man born in a large slum, and had somehow managed to go to school and had become a brilliant programmer. He was in the process of buying a flat for his large family. Abid's other friend, José, was a bright and ambitious young man from Rio who managed a small software division.

Abid's social network slowly came to consist of ex-pats who partied at bars and clubs, where the girls did not blush or talk of marriage. Gradually, he found bookshops, coffee shops, and pubs where he led a life that in some way resembled what he had been used to back in Canada.

****

A few months later, Abid called me up.

"I have two weeks for my vacation. I'm thinking of leaving India to work for Tata in South America or Europe. Why don't you come over before I leave and we'll go to Gujarat to track down our family"

"Just like that?"

"Well, you've talked about it often enough. You're getting on, you know."

He was right, of course, and Najma pushed me to go. She was teaching and could not accompany me.

My father had mentioned that the family farm was in a village close to the city of Rajkot and he had mentioned his full name as Hasham Velshi Khimji Pradhan, his given name followed by that of his immediate ancestors. I decided to use the city as the base for my search.

Najma suggested chatting with the Mukhi from our mosque. Generally a respected member of the congregation, the Mukhi, appointed by the Imam, is usually a businessman or professional, and he and his wife lead the congregation for a period of three years. The Mukhi, whose position most Ismailis covet, is a key figure in the informal local network. He is obliged to help a fellow Ismaili in any way. An Ismaili needing anything from temporary shelter in a new country to counseling in a marital dispute can approach the Mukhi or his wife.

I approached the Mukhi and was amazed at how much help and advice materialized. He put me in touch with four people who had recently been to Gujarat.

While chatting to the contacts, I discovered that I'd tapped into an extensive informal network connecting Ismailis who want to travel, volunteer, trace relatives, or even settle in another country. All the contacts the Mukhi gave me encouraged me to go to India and offered me names of relatives or friends who could help.

One of them, Jivraj, was the quintessential old-fashioned Ismaili entrepreneur. He was in the 'import-export' business, a trader always on the lookout for new business. When he smelled a demand for any product, he would ferret out the best supplier, anywhere in the world, and would then rush to meet the demand. When I got in touch with him, he said that clothes made in China were in great demand, so he was going there three times a year and would then stop over in Gujarat where he had friends and relatives. He gave me the most practical advice.

"You need a trustworthy driver and guide. I know just the man. His name is Abdulbhai. He owns a private taxi and he often acts as a guide for visitors for a week or two. Call him up and reserve him. Don't pay more than thirty dollars a day. Car insurance, everything, should be included. I'll drop him an e-mail. The best hotel to stay in is the Imperial – look it up on the Internet. I'll give you the name of the local Mukhi and also the phone number of my friend, Rajanbhai. He will give you a meal and sound advice, if you need it.

"Be careful. The minute you mention you are looking for *saggawallahs,* some people will put up their hands. Many locals are on the lookout for foreign relatives. They will find a connection to your family through some distant relationship - your father's second cousin's son. "Very close to your family," they will say. They all need help, perhaps an old mother, sickness in the family, or a son going to college. All good causes but how much can one man do? "

I called up Abdulbhai, the guide/taxi driver. He was available, sounded efficient and polite, took down my name, numbers and e-mail and asked me to give him the flight number as soon as possible. He promised to pick me up at the Rajkot airport.

****

A month later, I landed in Mumbai, around midnight.

Abid picked me up. He wore sandals, looked darker and had put on a little bit of weight and I was struck by how confident he appeared in handling the porters and his driver, shooing away anyone wanting to offer an unnecessary service. He got some money exchanged for me and bought me a bottle of water. He had arranged for me to stay close to his flat, at the Grand Hyatt, for a special rate. He had clearly learnt the Indian practice of getting the best value for our money. You have to bargain, especially if you are a tourist, Dad.

The taxi drove through the whiff of sewage that always seems to surround Mumbai airport and turned into a deserted side road that ended up at a gate. Three security men who ran scanners under the car, looked at my luggage, and demanded identification before opening the gate.

Inside, the hotel was welcoming, cool, modern, and spacious. Even at this hour, there were a few young men and women at and around the front desk, apparently waiting to answer any question, provide directions, and satisfy any reasonable need.

Abid left assuring me that he was okay to walk to his place at that time of night.

I was shown to a huge, ultramodern, air-conditioned room with a large flat screen TV. I crashed until Abid woke me up around midday, and we went down for brunch. It was a buffet catering to Northern and Southern Indian, as well as European tastes, with hot dishes and fresh-looking salads. We started with a glass of champagne – compliments of the management, sir.

Sated, Abid and I wandered through a delicate garden full of roses and bamboo, with a little gushing stream. It seemed like a tranquil Japanese space. We walked out through the gates towards his home, and within fifty yards of the Hyatt's walled-in compound, we ran into a slum.

It was a small slum, with perhaps a dozen tin and three-ply thatched shelters, a couple of cows and some children running around. Still trying to grapple with the sudden change, I watched Abid chatting with two little boys, one in his underwear, and a little girl in a torn dirty dress. They followed him for a while and then turned to me and held out their hands. I looked at Abid. He nodded, and I took out some notes. He picked out a ten.

"What we just spent on that brunch would take their family three months to make," he said, with a slight smile and his sardonic tone.

Thanks, Abid, I replied wryly conscious of the rich meal in my stomach.

When we got close to the end of the street, he pointed to his flat nestled somewhere in a group of half a dozen large, older apartment buildings. At the entrance of his complex was a jumble of tiny shops. He picked up his laundry and introduced me to Chandu, the *dhobi* who washed his clothes once a week, and Mr. Nayyar, owner of a local convenience store from whom he bought me a bottle of water.

"It's a good safe brand. Never drink tap water," he said as he handed it to me.

We walked up to his eighth-floor apartment, a small, cluttered space, like a student dorm. One of his friends, Stephen, a young man from Athens, was watching the news. He slept on a pull out. The rest of the occupants were out, and as we walked slowly through the flat, Abid pointed out where everyone slept until we ended up at the balcony, a reasonably large one with chicken-coup wire covering most of it.

"The wire stops the pigeons entering and pooping all over the balcony," Abid told me.

"So where's your bedroom?" I asked.

"This is it," he said, pointing to the sleeping bag on the balcony floor.

"What do you mean?"

"Well, it's quiet and warm after midnight, the monsoon is over and I can watch the sunrise and listen to the *azaan* from that minaret in the morning. It's actually quite comfortable – in fact, spectacular."

"Look, I can easily supplement your rent, Abid."

"Don't worry, dad, I chose this. I'm only going to be here for a few weeks. The other advantage is it's close to the Santa Cruz station. In fact, I'd planned for us to go downtown by train. It'll be quiet at this time."

We walked down to the station, and a man behind a small stall hailed him.

"How are you, Abid sahib?"

Mahendra, the food vendor, served sandwiches, samosas and other Indian snacks. His stall was neat and the food looked tasty.

"I've already had my breakfast," said Abid.

Other than the fact that he spoke in English, he seemed to be perfectly at home.

When we arrived on the platform, he steered me away from the *zenana* car towards a mixed-gender compartment.

"The women in *burkha* or those who want to just be with other women have their own car. Safety for women is a big problem," he explained.

Our car was a very bare affair – steel benches with worn-out surfaces, and other than that, just standing room.

We sat on one of the benches, and as the train chugged forward, we watched the grimy tenements and little workshops that lined the tracks.

"Tell me about your average day," I asked.

"I buy a tea and usually an egg sandwich, a safe meal, from Mahendra and push my way into the train."

"Push?"

"Well, that's the safe way. Some people hang out of the doors. Some even get on the top of the trains – the ones that don't want to pay the fares. It's completely crazy. It's nothing like the trains back home or in Europe, where there are rules, here it's everyone for themselves."

"But you manage to get on and off with no problem?"

"Well, I had one interesting experience, but you might not like to hear about it," he smiled.

"Well, you might as well tell me. I'm in adjustment mode."

"A few weeks ago, I went clothes shopping downtown. Thought I'd buy some nice Indian *kurta* shirts and stuff. So after shopping, I board the southern most station, Victoria. As we go towards Santa Cruz, new passengers get on, and I keep getting pushed back. Finally, I'm almost crushed against the back doors. At Santa Cruz, I just can't get out. Suddenly, the back door opens, I look out, and I don't know what gets into my head . . . It looks empty, so I jump out.

"I land feet first, hands full of shopping – straight into a pile of poop. The street and some slum people treat the space around the railway tracks as a massive, open-air toilet.

"Suddenly, I realize that people are yelling at me, pointing behind me. I turn and see a train coming straight at me. People swarm to the edge and haul me over."

I looked at him, and became a believer for the moment and said a prayer of gratitude to the One up there.

There was nothing I could do. He was in charge of his life, and he was going to lead it the way he wanted to. It's easy to tell them to explore the world, difficult to live with the reality. I still carry memories of bringing him home from the hospital, helping him learn how to walk, and teaching him how to ride a bike.

"So what about dating? You going out with anyone?"

"I tried dating Indian girls . . . It's too complicated."

"What do you mean?"

"Well, the first one I dated made it clear at the very beginning: "My parents want me to get married in a year,' she said."

"Hmmm."

Then I tried it a second time.

"Yes?"

"She started to e-mail me like crazy and kept coming over to the cubicle. Took me a while to dissuade her."

"What do you do in the evenings?"

"Other than a couple of Indian friends, I hang out with ex-pat kids mostly – we'll meet them – and I have an Australian friend that I volunteer for."

"What sort of volunteering?"

"She runs a street kids program, and I teach the kids English. The kids hang around railway stations, and they all want to learn English. Many are new to the city and most have no place to live.

"They arrive with dreams of becoming Bollywood stars or just to escape from home, from parents who want to put them to work. They end up in the slums. The lucky ones get jobs in sweat shops, become servants, sell stuff on the streets and the unlucky ones end up as prostitutes or beggars, but almost no one will go back.

"Anyway, we take them to a park at Bombay University, play ball and teach them English. Most of them are so keen to learn. Sometimes I take my PC. I do that once a week. It's a pretty incredible experience.

Do you know a thousand people come to this city every day? A thousand. How many come to Toronto, I wonder?"

"A thousand a day makes it over three hundred and fifty thousand a year. Canada takes in maybe two hundred thousand, usually pretty educated" I replied.

"That's for the whole of Canada," said Abid, shaking his head. "This is one city."

I was impressed with what he'd already learned in a few months of living in India. We could not possibly have given him a better education at home. No books, lectures, or movies could have taught him to understand the Indian culture or to appreciate living amongst people who fought so fiercely for a little breathing space and put in long hours to earn a single dollar. Perhaps more importantly he learned that people who live in dire straits in slums and on the streets still maintain dignity and a sense of community.

****

That evening, we left our cool hotel to meet some of his friends. They were from Turkey, South America, Greece, Ireland, Poland and the United States. To me they seemed wonderful young people, adventurous, willing to work or volunteer in one of the most overcrowded spaces in the world and mostly unable to speak any local language. They were made up of two groups. There were those working for large multinationals, earning a reasonable salary and had come to understand how business was done in India. The other group was made up of social activists, who had set up their own NGOs or were working for charities. I was struck by their empathy for the poor and the dispossessed.

The boomer generation to which I belong was politicized, protested against colonization, opposed the war in Vietnam, and marched for civil rights when they were young. They created rock music and experimented with drugs and free love. But these young people often worked alone or in small groups for extremely low wages, with little recognition and tremendous passion. It seemed to me that this generation, unlike the passionate idealists of my generation, was the one that practiced quiet and invaluable action.

I had a couple of beers and a few kebabs, and then took a taxi back to the hotel to recover from my jet lag while Abid stayed on.

****

The next day we explored the city, splurged a little, and enjoyed some of the delights of Mumbai. We started with Haji Ali Mosque.

The mosque is built at the end of a spit of land that juts out into the Arabian Sea and is accessible only when the tide is out. It is said that in the fifteenth century, a rich Muslim merchant, Ali Shah Bukhari, died on his way to Mecca during the pilgrimage to Mecca, the Hajj. His body, cast out to sea, floated back to this point on the Mumbai shoreline where his *dargah* was built.

On Fridays at midday, a group of qwaals sings Sufi qualaam. The powerful singing, usually by men in a call and response style, reminds me of Negro spiritual music. It is focused on the power of the voice and poetry and accompanied by just a *peti* (an accordion on the floor) and *tablas* and *drums*. These men are often Sunni but they sing in praise of Ali, the first Imam of the Shia. The Sufis, including the Turkish ones who perform whirling dances, are the only Muslims I know that permit music, singing and dancing in their prayers. Almost all other forms of Islam consider music during prayers to be Haraam, forbidden.

Abid and I bought cold cokes and some hot potato fritters, walked to the end of the spit where there was a thick low wall and sat down to listen to the master musicians. Against the sound of the sea lapping against the smooth, ink black rocks surrounding the mosque, they sang with absolute abandon. The poetry, the sound of music and the surf, melded into a magical and hypnotic concert.

After the performance ended we took a walk close to the sea along Dr Annie Besant Road, named after the Englishwoman who joined the fight for Indian independence. This thin strip of affluence, between the road and the sea, is where the wealthiest and most influential citizens of Mumbai live in apartments facing the ocean. To the south, the business district and the university are clustered along this strip, and to the north are upscale neighbourhoods like Juhu and Bandra, where the film stars live. The long strip probably houses a large portion of the economic and cultural power of not just Mumbai, but of India. In the hinterland lie swaths of tenements, slums, and pockets of middle-class homes.

The disparity between rich and poor in this city is probably the most pronounced of any place I've ever visited. People who barely earn a hundred rupees -two dollars- a day, live side-by-side with people who earn six-figure incomes. Surprisingly, there appears to be little anger or resentment on the part of the poor. They say that the rich have good *naseeb* and that to be born rich is a gift from Bhagwan. The rich, on the other hand, generally have little respect for the masses and ignore the poor except their cooks, guards, and housemaids and the retinues of other servants who look after them.

It was getting hot and customers began to mill around the coconut vendors who were busy lopping off the green coconut heads with sharp knives and pouring out the sweet water. Their two-wheel carts looked out of place beside the entrance of a mall adorned with promises of Versace and Cartier. Abid guided me to an air-conditioned salon with a parlour full of magazines, a cappuccino machine, and three solid old-fashioned American-style barber chairs. He knew Jitu the sophisticated hairdresser who recommended an old-fashioned shave and massage for me. Abid had a quick shave and read a magazine while a young man quickly lathered my face, gave me a smooth, close shave, wrapped my face in a hot towels, and then proceeded to massage my neck and upper back. He had been doing this for ten years and was good at it. "I come from Bihar," he told me. Bihar is probably the poorest, least educated state of India. The massage and shave, a deliciously refreshing experience, had lasted for an hour and a half and cost fifteen dollars for the two of us.

We decided to cap the day with a visit to the Taj Hotel, where Najma and I had stayed that January of '93 when violence had erupted just outside its opulent doors. The hotel had become even more expensive and luxurious in the intervening years. The locals now dominated a place that had been full of foreigners twelve years before. We ordered beer and settled down to watch a stream of guests coming in for a wedding reception.

A Hindu wedding, especially for the rich, is a unique and colourful spectacle. I started to talk to the waiter who told us that this party was the last celebration of the wedding before the bride and groom could take off for their honeymoon and some privacy.

The Hindu wedding consists of several ceremonies – one held the day before, the actual wedding, a tearful farewell as the bride departs from the bosom of her family (with the understanding that she will not return), and then the bride's reception into the family of the in-laws (who would be counting on a substantial dowry). Among wealthy families, the entire process can take a full week.

I have a good idea of what likely went on during the wedding from attending Hindu weddings as a boy in Nairobi. The marriage ceremony takes place around a fire. It goes on for hours and seems to be designed to wear out the bride and bridegroom, not to mention the guests. The

Brahmin priest who conducts the ceremony is showered with gifts and cash for putting everyone through the ordeal. At the end there is the long, spicy, meal usually fried and accompanied by super sweet desserts.

Abid and I watched the parade of the women in blazing *sarees* embroidered with gold or silver and men in long *sherwanis*, the fine *churiddars*, and embroidered *mojris* covering their feet. Some of the crowd was dressed in the latest Italian or Parisian haute couture.

My stomach had been acting up, so I decided to visit the washroom, one of the cleanest that I knew of in the city.

Two young boys in wedding clothes were heading over to the urinal area. I settled down on the throne and listened to the boys.

"*Yaar,* when my mum told me there was going to be another wedding, I was sooo mad."

"I know what you mean – we have to wear these stupid clothes."

"I can't get this *sali naadi* [damn drawstring] untied!"

"I know. They're a pain. And then I can't get it out, and I sometimes piss on these *mojris*.

"This is stupid. When I get married, we'll go to Goa and just do it."

"So, you're still seeing Rohini, huh?"

Then someone pulled the flush lever.

When I came out, a tall, well-dressed man in a long, black *sherwani* was standing around. I wondered if he was a wedding guest. But when I washed my hands, he suddenly produced a towel and handed it over to me ceremoniously. I realized he was the towel-*wallah*, but I didn't know whether I should give him a tip. I gave him a few rupees, and a small smile flitted across his face. I wondered what he was thinking.

Abid and I adjourned to one of the restaurants in the Taj and ordered a chicken *biriyani* and eggplant curry. I enjoyed the live sitar performance while Abid enjoyed the meal. There was a fair bit of food left over, and Abid asked for it to be packed up. I wondered when he was going to eat it, as he was having all his meals with me. Outside, I walked slowly, enjoying the warm evening while he moved ahead of me. He stopped in front of a man with unkempt hair covered in a filthy blanket, sitting immobile on the street too weak to beg or even look up.

Is the man asleep? Why is Abid standing in front of him? Abid put the package in front of him. The man slowly raised his head and blessed him in a low voice: "May Allah keep you happy, *beta*."

His grandmother's teaching passed on through his mother – spend on what you need for today, save some for tomorrow, and share with those who have nothing.

9. Roots in Gujarat.

Abdul, the driver, was waiting for us with a placard at Rajkot airport. It had been just over an hour's flight north of Mumbai and from what I had heard of it, the four hundred year old historical city was reputed to be popular with tourists, lively, full of gardens, forts and palaces. If I did not manage to get any information about my father's family, Abid and I would hopefully enjoy the city.

Abdul was in his fifties, a stocky, soft-spoken, graying man. We asked him to take us to a *jalebi* and *ganthia* shop. He smiled, pleased and amused at our request for the traditional Gujarati favourite. The sweet pretzel and the long flour strips, both fried, served with fried green chillies, spicy, shredded carrots and cabbage was a delicacy my father had loved as I do now. Abid enjoys them once in a while.

When I talked about local food, Abdul promised to take me somewhere later for a peasant meal with *rotlas*. My father taught me to make this millet flatbread, eaten with garlic, chillies, and yogourt. Abid has no taste for them. I usually make a pile of them while I drink a couple of glasses of Chardonnay and mess up Najma's kitchen.

That evening Abid and I took our passports to the local liquor store to buy some Indian beer. Gujarat is a dry state and still requires foreigners to identify themselves with a passport and enough paperwork to discourage you from returning to the store. We also tried an Indian wine, which turned out to be atrocious.

The next evening we went to the main jamatkhanna, the usual two-storied rectangular stone building that took me back to a cool Friday evening in Nairobi, when my mother or grandmother took me to the prayer hall of the main mosque. The women covered their heads, the air was filled with the smell of incense and food offerings and the congregation sat on a concrete floor covered with a thin straw mat. I've always wondered why I have to sit on that hard uncomfortable surface as I pray to the almighty. Now that I am older, I can sit on a chair if I choose to but I've not accepted that privilege yet and so I silently suffer through discomfort.

After the service, we asked around for people who might know our family. The only people who had any memories of the old days were elderly women. We came across Jenabai, a slim woman with green eyes wearing a light blue sari. She had dignity and presence and must have been a stunning beauty in her younger days. In her soft, mellow voice, she told us that she remembered a family that seemed to match my description and whose patriarch was an imperious man whom she said I resembled. This was the second time someone said I possibly looked like my grandfather.

The first person who pointed out the resemblance was Najma's maternal grandfather.

****

The only time I met Najma's grandparents was when she took me to their home in Moshi, a small town on the slopes of Mount Kilimanjaro in Tanzania. We were preparing to emigrate; I remember the visit in vivid detail.

It was a warm brilliantly sunny day and the snow capped Kilimanjaro was clearly visible. We walked up to the third floor of a low-rise apartment building in the centre of town and knocked on the door. It creaked open a few inches, and a bespectacled face peered out. It took her grandfather a few moments to recognize Najma and then we were ushered in quickly. Tea was immediately prepared and d*ubbas* full of *chevdo, purees* and biscuits flew open. Her grandmother Sambai, a small woman with short grey hair dyed in henna, was in tears. She reminded me of my grandmother, dressed in the long frock with a pachedi on her head.

As I tucked in, her grandfather looked at me and said, "You are the spitting image of Velshi Khimji. I recognized you at once."

Najma and I looked at each other in surprise. It somehow gave me great satisfaction, a sense of validation, that I resembled my grandfather.

Hassam Jessa then explained why it had taken him so long to open the door. Government officials had seized the entire apartment building that the family had owned prior to the nationalization of 1973, except for the apartment they were now living in. Since the officials considered it spacious they were now looking to move another family into apartment.

After independence in Tanzania, its president, Julius Nyerere, started a massive and ambitious socialist program. Businesses were the first to be nationalized. The Jessas, who previously owned a farm in the foothills of Mount Kilimanjaro, had finally sold it because they were no longer able to manage it. Their children had all migrated to the West. With the proceeds of the sale the old couple paid off the mortgage on the apartment block in Moshi, which they had built for their retirement and moved into one flat, hoping to live off the rent of the remaining units. A few months later, the apartment building was nationalized and they were allocated one flat to live in.

Initially devastated, they became philosophical about their loss.

"We came from India with nothing, and now at least we have this apartment," Sambai said, "We've lived a wonderful life."

After migrating from India, Sambai and Hassam had worked hard and saved money with which they had bought a tract of bush land in the foothills of Mount Kilimanjaro, cleared it, built a reservoir, and started a mixed dairy and fruit farm.

Najma was born in Moshi and spent her school vacations there. Her memories are vivid, of the Maasai who came to trade blankets and skins for sugar and flour and cooking oil, of the starry night against which Kilimanjaro stood with its white peak visible and of the family who raucously played cards on blankets spread out in the living room lit by kerosene lamps. She particularly remembers the orchard on the farm, which produced a profusion of fruit, including oranges, mangoes, and bananas. When the unpicked pomegranates fell to the ground, the cows, that loved to snack on the cracked ones, were allowed to amble through the orchard, crunching them before gobbling them up.

And she still talks of Amin, her older cousin, who piled them into the back of the Bedford pick-up and took them hunting for Dik-Dik or Thomson's gazelle. Amin's father had died in a gun accident.

Najma describes travelling, usually in late afternoon, over a labyrinth of dirt tracks on the Savannah close to the farm. If they got lost, Amin would climb on the top of the car to figure out their bearings. When they shot an animal, they took it home and skinned it, and the women made curries, samosas and barbecues. The barbecues were pits dug into the ground with a bed of burning coal at the bottom. The skewered meat was placed between the bed and a wire mesh at ground level, which was also covered with burning coals. Basted with green chilli chutney, coriander, and yogourt, the meat was left to cook slowly and started to fall off the bone when it was cooked to perfection.

Both our maternal grandmothers had, in many respects, led similar lives. Both married at fourteen, bore a dozen or so children, some of whom were delivered with the help of friends before there were midwives around. It seemed to me that the women really were the stronger partners in the marriages. Both were barely five feet tall and ran big households, worked in the shops and farms, and traded with the local tribesmen and persuaded them to occasionally become hired help. My grandparents had settled and lived for many years in a small town called Machakos before moving to Nairobi in Kenya. Nanima helped run a small general store which sold goods to the Wakamba tribe and learned Kiswahili, Kikuyu, and Wakamba, enough to get along and curse the servants, who loved her anyway.

Najma's grandparents' idyllic existence came to an end with the declaration of independence and the introduction of President Nyerere's policies of African socialism. The policy led to an exodus of the Asians including Najma's aunts, uncles, and cousins who got dispersed throughout Kenya, Canada, and the United Kingdom.

I sat with Najma's grandfather while Sambai took her through to the rest of apartment. They reminisced and Najma picked out a few pictures from the old albums and a beautiful old piece of fabric that her grandmother insisted she take.

Hassam Jessa talked of the old days, the utter stupidity of the government, his mood swinging between sadness and fury. I doubted if he would ever get over the loss of his farm and the apartments.

I thought of asking him where he had met my grandfather but doubted if he would remember the details. He must have been quite young then. I decided I could pursue the matter after we settled in Canada by writing to him.

We said our goodbyes amid tears, and I still remember how Hassam and Sambai held each other as they waved to us from the balcony. They died within months of each other soon after we arrived in Canada.

A year later Amin was killed, like his father by a crop-destroying elephant.

****

The elderly lady at the Rajkot mosque spoke in the same cadence, using the same expressions as our grandparents. She told me that my grandfather's farm had probably been in a village not far from Rajkot, but she had no idea where the family was now. Probably moved to Pakistan during the Partition, she suggested. She gave us the names of some people who might have known them.

Over the next few days we drove into several villages, one village after another, and attempted to track down the people whose names we had been given. The dusty roads ran through the arid countryside but occasionally we came upon surprising patches of green farmland. The people were small and dark, the men wore large turbans and the women faded cotton saris with intricate designs.

Abdulbhai had become more relaxed with us and explained the feelings of local Gujarati Muslims towards Narendra Modi, the Chief Minister. Many Hindus thought of him as the CEO of their state, since he'd brought them efficiency, infrastructure, and jobs, but the Muslims largely hated and feared him especially after the Godhra affair.

In 2002 a train was forcibly stopped at a station called Godhra and attacked by a large mob of Muslim fanatics. About 60 Hindu pilgrims – mostly women, children, and seniors returning from the holy city of Ayodhya – were burned alive. In retaliation, the Hindus began massacring Muslims on a large scale. About a thousand people, mostly Muslim, were killed in the riots. Hundreds of homes, places of worship, and businesses were burned down. According to Abdulbhai, the government of Modi stood by, refused to intervene, and encouraged the revenge. Three years later, not surprisingly, relations between Muslims and Hindus in Gujarat were still extremely tense.

Back in Rajkot, word of our search spread quickly, and a man called me up to inform me that he believed that his mother was a cousin of my father's and invited us for tea to his home. We went to visit Jamil, a tall thin, dark, handsome, moustachioed man, with deep shiny eyes. He laboured in a small factory and lived in a tiny cinder block house with two bright children and a large cylindrical wife who immediately bent down to touch my feet, a Hindu gesture of respect for an elder. I was more taken aback by her flexibility and speed in performing that act than anything else. I blessed her, as I was expected to do, and she brought out tea and snacks. Their son, eleven-year-old Nasir, was obviously an intelligent boy. He took our camera, which was giving us some trouble, fixed it within minutes and then started talking enthusiastically about his school. He was at the top of his class, his proud father told us, and needed to move on to a higher grade but the school fees were too high for the family to afford.

Jamil took us to meet his mother, Sakinabai, and the rest of the family. We were introduced as relatives from Canada; two chickens were bought live from a nearby market and slaughtered. Sakinabai supervised her two daughters-in-law as they cooked what turns turned out to be a delicious curry. We ate it with mounds of rice and slices of white bread. Eight people came to visit and dine with us. The men, mostly taxi drivers, went back to work after lunch.

Five of us were left, sitting cross-legged on a concrete floor covered with a straw mat. I was closest to the wall and could lean against it, a privilege for an honoured guest. Abid was sitting next to me but did not lean back. Sakinabai, in a plain, light green sari, sat opposite me, flanked by her older son, Salim, and his pretty daughter Azmina. Thin, with a wizened face and sparse grey hair, Sakinabai had lively and inquisitive eyes behind her thick spectacles.

As the matriarch of the family, she seemed to be very much in charge and deeply respected. Her husband had left her this tiny flat in the Ismaili colony in Rajkot, and she was sharing it with Salim, his wife and their daughter.

Clearing her throat she looked at me. I guessed that this would be the start of the first level of information gathering about my background, a quintessentially Indian introduction.

Unexpectedly, she started with Abid.

"So what do you do, *beta?*"

"I work in Mumbai, in the computer business, for a big software company."

Since Abid does not speak the language, Azmina translated.

"Oh, it's all beyond me, but I hear it's very lucrative. But aren't you from Canada?"

"I am here just for an internship."

Again a translation.

"You come from that far to learn all this in India?"

"Yes, I am learning a lot."

"*Shabash,*" she said, praising him, and turned turned to me: "And you have other family?"

"My wife, Najma, and our daughter Sameena."

"Is she married?"

"Oh, no. She is just starting her college."

"These days many girls go to college. Our Azmina here is also going to college. She is studying Bijnuss."

Azmina, the business student, has been eyeing Abid, and he has been studiously avoiding her.

Now Abid is handsome – a catch – even if I do say so myself.

Sakinabai turns to me.

"But you live in Canada?"

"Yes, in a city called Toronto."

"This is your first visit?"

"No, actually my third."

"But first to Rajkot?"

"Yes."

"I hear you are looking for your *dada*."
"Yes. Did you know him?"
"What was the name again?"
"Velshi Khimji. I heard him say we were Piranis."
"A Pirani is of our clan. Was he from Phulkot?"
" I don't know. All I know is that Rajkot was the closest town."
"Many of the Piranis come from the village of Phulkot. I can't remember well. I was a young woman. But there was Khimji Bhai, tall like you with a moustache and resembled you. Rode a horse, liked to dress well, erect, a man of few words. One of his sons had run away. To Africa?"

She did not add that Khimji Bhai was a goodhearted man, a common courtesy description applied to the departed. I had also sensed from my father that my grandfather was an autocratic, hard man.

"My father went to Africa from around here," I replied. "I was born in Kenya. Do you know if any of my Dada's family is still there? Maybe I can go to the village – Phulkot?"

"No, no. The whole village was taken over by Hindus during the Partition. They might suspect that you are trying to claim the land or looking for compensation. Too dangerous."

"So you are Piranis too. Are you my father's cousin? "

"I don't think so. I think we may be distantly related."

I looked around for Jamil, who has claimed this close relationship. He was avoiding eye contact, playing with the children in another corner of the room.

"Whether you are closely related or not, you are always welcome."

Sakinabai passed a bottle of *Suva dana*, a mixture of seeds-dill, sesame, and coriander seeds sprinkled with sugar-coated anisette, an addictive after-dinner offering, supposed to aid digestion that is jokingly referred to as *java dana* – goodbye seeds.

One does not immediately get up but slowly prepares to depart after this signal.

We were all quiet for a few moments as we slowly chewed the delicious concoction.

Sakinabai spoke slowly and thoughtfully.

"Most probably your father's family would have gone to Pakistan. I know terrible things happened to people during the Partition, and if they survived, they might be in the colonies around the Garden Jamat Khanna in Karachi. Go to the Mukhi there and make enquiries."

Was I ready to go to Karachi? The port city lay a few hundred miles to the northwest and since we were not too far, perhaps it was worth considering going there.

"Consider yourself *nasibdar* to have such good fortune. Your father left early for Africa and escaped the Partition, and we stayed behind. That is the only difference between you and us. And look at you now and look at us."

There is a tinge of regret in her voice, I thought, for not having taken a chance and gone to Africa.

After we left the colony, Abid and I decided that there wasn't much more information to be gained in Rajkot. With a few days of the trip still left I began to think on Sakinbai's advice to follow the family to Pakistan.

"Let's go to Karachi, Abid" I said.

"It's a couple of hours' flight from here," he replied, "but we need to go to Delhi first, to get visas. It'll be frustrating and take a lot of time. There are so many problems between the two countries. It's easier to get visas from Toronto. We can always come back, maybe next year. We have to."

V. RETURN TO MUMBAI

"Spread your thumb and your forefinger apart at a thirty degree angle and you'll see the shape of Mumbai – you'll find yourself acknowledging that it is a beautiful city: the sea on all sides, the palm trees along the shores, the lights coming down from the sky and thrown back up by the sea. It has a harbour, several bays, creeks, rivers and hills. From the air, you get a sense of all its possibilities. On the ground, it's different."

Maximum City: Bombay Lost and Found by Suketu Mehta

10. An Inner-city School, Mumbai, 2009.

The board on the shop said, "Fakr-ud-deen Fancy Goods Store."

We had endured an hour in a rattling old taxi to get from Colaba to Byculla, a poor, predominantly Muslim, inner-city district of Mumbai. We had left the seaside neighbourhood of luxury hotels, large glossy modern offices, the quaint old Colaba street market, shops and restaurants catering to tourists and the wealthy locals and found ourselves in a mass of old low-rise apartment buildings and tiny shops that sold basic necessities on a narrow sidewalk used for all manners of individual enterprise. It was a sobering change.

We were on our way to visit two schools with the aim of choosing one to volunteer at, but first we had to find a place to purchase mobile phone credit.

The large sign outside the store that said "Vodaphone dealer" attracted us.

The shopkeeper, presumably Fakr-ud-deen, was a tall, thin, almost bald man with a scraggly goatee. His spectacles rested below the bridge of his nose as he peered down at Najma.

"We'd like to recharge our phone," Najma started.

"What phone company, Madum?"

"Vodaphone."

"No problem. How much?"

Najma glanced at me.

"A thousand rupees," I replied.

"A tousand?" he said, sounding surprised.

No one in this neighbourhood would recharge for that much, I guessed. I was still thinking in terms of Canadian dollars and I'd estimated that twenty-five dollars should last us a couple of weeks. We needed the large credit mostly to call Abid and Sameena and some business associates in Canada.

A little flustered, Fakr-ud-deen shouted, "Adnan!"

Adnan, a heavy-set young man, came in from the back of the store, looking exasperated with Fakr-ud-deen. He welcomed us and took our phone.

"They need to charge for a tousand."

"We can do it, Papa. Break it up into two five-hundred charges."

They spoke to each other in Gujarati.

While Adnan was handling the order, Fakr-ud-deen asked, " Where are you from?"

And when I answered, "Gujarat", he immediately responded, "Kem Cho?"

The stock answer to the question, 'How are you?' is "Majama." Even in the direst of circumstances, this is the answer to give, "I am happy."

Sensing that I wasn't the real deal, the inquiry continued: "NRI (Non Resident Indian) from Africa?"

Somehow, Fakr-ud-deen had managed to recognize us easily; something about our air, accent and attire had given us away.

"Yes, but moved to Canada many years ago."

"Nice country but cold, no?"

The question of my origins, surprisingly, continued to dog me more in India than in Canada.

In India the question 'Where are you from?' usually means, which of the thirty-five states are you from?

An Indian name is a unique label. It often discloses one's religion- Hindu, Muslim, Christian or Sikh. In the case of the Hindus, it also often identifies the caste one belongs to. The State where one comes from establishes the language that one is most likely to speak. Identifying individuals by religion, caste and language remain a fundamental part of the Indian psyche, one that is ever-present, though never publicly acknowledged.

In Canada, I'm often asked, "Where do you come from?"

When I say "Kenya", the eyes say, "But you' re not black. You look Indian or Middle Eastern or something."

"I was born in Africa. Originally from India," I usually add.

"Aaah! Now I understand," the eyes say.

Elsewhere in the world, I usually say, "I'm from Canada. Originally Indian." I skip the part about Kenya. It gets too cumbersome to explain it all.

By now I could tell from his accent and his name that Fakr-ud-deen was a Bohra Muslim. The Bohras speak Gujarati with a distinct accent, and other Gujarati-speaking Indians tease Bohras because of their inability to distinguish between *th* and *t*. Hence a thousand becomes a "tousand" and the number three becomes a "tree."

We asked Fakru-ud-deen where the Aga Khan School was.

"You are Aga Khannies?" he asked. The Ismailis are often referred to by that name in India.

"Yes," we replied.

"You are going to teach there?"

"We hope to volunteer there."

"Welcome, welcome. My son Adnan's children, a boy and a girl, go there. The school is just round the corner."

We knew that "just round the corner" could mean many things in India, and seeing that we were unsure, Fakr-ud-deen left the shop, walked with us down the street, and pointed to the entrance of the school.

We shook hands and thanked him.

"Come for tea during recess. You are welcome any time. We are related after all," he said.

By saying we were related, he was referring to the fact that the Ismailis and the Bohras once belonged to the same Shia sect.

"Tell me how the Ismailis and Bohras split," I asked Najma as we walked away.

Najma, having consumed many thick volumes of Ismaili history, has now become the resident expert within the circle of our friends and family.

"I'll give you a Reader's Digest version," said Najma. "You know something about the Fatimids."

I nodded. At the peak of their power, the Ismaili Fatimid Imams, ruled Egypt and established the city of Cairo as their capital.

She continued: "One of the Fatimid Imams, Mustansir Billah, had two sons: Nizar, the older one, and his younger brother, Mustali. The followers of Nizar became Nizari Ismailis and the followers of Mustali became known as the Bohras. Both these groups came to India and converted Fake-ud-deen's and our ancestors."

As we stood in front of the school, I thought back to how this undertaking started almost three months ago in Toronto. I've never been inclined to do one thing at a time and since I had to travel on a work-related assignment to India, I began to think of other opportunities for my time there.

Najma and I had often talked about volunteering in India. I suggested to her that we also travel to parts of India that we hadn't visited during our previous three trips. We've been married long enough that she accepts this proclivity to overextend myself. I knew she'd slow me down and start to organize what could realistically be achieved.

"It will take us at least two months to do all this," she observed.

I knew my workload would decrease after this visit while the company planned the next steps, and I could continue to be involved in the planning from India through the Internet. We would leave in early January and come back sometime in late March. In any case, I didn't want to return to Canada in the middle of winter.

"So this time we can't go as tourists. We can't afford to do that for two months. We should live in B&Bs, take public transport or local taxis or even three wheeler tuk-tuks, and eat like the locals," said Najma

"If you really want to experience India," Sameena agreed, "that's what you should do, Dad."

She started to help us organize our trip. By now, at twenty, she was a well-travelled young woman. She had taken off to India for two months, in part because Abid's experiences had intrigued her and partly because she was curious about her own Indianness. She travelled over three thousand miles on buses and trains, in overcrowded third class compartments and lived in hostels and cheap hotels. During most of the trip, two Italian friends, Lulu and Isabella, accompanied her but for a few weeks, a fearful time for us, she was on her own.

She covered a huge part of India; walking along the ghats on river Ganges in the holy city of Varanasi, exploring the French quarter of Pondicherry on a bike, ordering a seafood barbecue from fishermen on the beaches of Cochin and volunteering in a hostel run by Mother Theresa's organization in Mumbai. Through many nights I lay awake worrying about her while she was travelling or living alone. I felt twinges of regret in having encouraged her to travel the world. As it was for Abid, the trip became an unforgettable experience and education; it gave her an appreciation of her roots and how privileged a life she led.

Both she and Abid recommended the latest copy of *Lonely Planet India*.

"Just pick the moderately priced accommodation and you'll be fine, Dad. We've lived in the inexpensive ones. You wouldn't last in them."

Outnumbered I agreed but, Najma and I knew that there would be further negotiations in India. This is an ongoing little battleground for us. I prefer four- and five-star establishments, but Najma would rather live much more modestly but she knew my aversion to cheap lodgings that could remind me of the one-room flats I had spent my childhood in.

****

My assignment, for a large Canadian multinational, was made up of two parts. The first was to understand the real estate industry in India, particularly services such as brokerage, and the second was to look for outsourcing of accounting and other operations currently being done by my client in Canada.

We decided that Najma would meet me at the end of my trip, probably in Bangalore. This was my fourth trip to India and Najma's third. We'd already travelled to the more popular areas of Delhi, Rajasthan, Mumbai, Gujarat, and Goa during previous trips. We tentatively planned to travel the route that Sameena had followed before settling down in Mumbai, where we'd likely volunteer.

While I started planning all the details of my visit with a business colleague, Najma got going on organizing the rest of our trip. She sought out reasonable accommodation, the sights to see, upcoming concerts, and the art galleries to visit, particularly in Mumbai and Calcutta. Galleries would be a priority because she wanted to explore the art scene in India. She paints in oils, a passion that has taken up all her spare time since she retired the year before we left for Mumbai.

Fatima, a close friend of ours in Toronto, gave us the name of someone who could help us arrange our volunteering in Mumbai for the AKDN (The Aga Khan Development Network). I had heard a lot about the organization but knew very little about how it operated. I decided to do some research and was taken aback.

AKDN operates 250 schools and universities in Africa, Central Asia, India and Pakistan. It also runs over 300 hospitals, as well as other projects, including providing microcredit for women to start small businesses and building hydroelectric power stations. Some of these projects are huge and others small but always built with heavy involvement of the community or government they are intended to serve. Initially focused on helping the followers of the Aga Khan living in East Africa and the Indian subcontinent, the AKDN now operates in twenty-five countries.

I was struck by the fact that it employs sixty thousand people, as many as the Royal bank. Many Ismailis who have migrated to Canada and other Western countries volunteer for the AKDN overseas, as do their children.

The Aga Khan, who oversees all of these operations, is an unusual man, as is the eclectic set of agencies he oversees. The spiritual leader is a Harvard-educated entrepreneur and philanthropist who lives in Paris, and his role is the subject of curiosity, controversy, and admiration in the Islamic world. He is very wealthy in his own right; he races horses, skis, travels in his own jet, and is in general nothing like the notion of a spiritual leader in any other Islamic sect or, for that matter, any other religion.

Fatima's contact put us in touch with Salim, a senior officer of administration at AKES (Aga Khan Educational Services). We emailed him our résumés, which he passed on to the principals of schools that might be interested in our services and even offered to help us look for accommodation. He suggested a moderately priced option, a YMCA close to the schools, which the AKES frequently used for putting up visiting teachers and where we would get a good room at a special price.

****

I was part of a team that spent ten days talking to consultants, senior civil servants, entrepreneurs and established businessmen, collecting information and identifying possible partners to do business with in the future. The difference in the India of 1993 and the India of 2009 was astounding.

Higher education, though still only available to a small segment of the population, combined with entrepreneurship and government encouragement of private sector investment had transformed the economy and created a burgeoning middle class. The expertise, confidence and insights displayed by the people we talked to was truly impressive. We visited three cities, Delhi, Mumbai and Bangalore, lived in five star hotels, ate rich food and worked fourteen hours a day.

With a notebook full of information, I parted company with my team in Bangalore and found myself in a small bed and breakfast that Najma had booked for us. Sitting in its small garden, on a lush lawn and surrounded by paw paw trees, jasmine and rose bushes, we went through a list of places Najma had made, predominantly in Western and Central India that had intrigued us from what we had read or heard of their history or cultural significance.

It was not going to be the kind of journey, with a planned itinerary, we usually made. We chose a city, booked a flight, hotel, train or a rental car with a driver one or two days ahead of travelling and arranged the next stop using the phone, the Internet and the Lonely Planet as our guide. At first, this lack of a plan, felt uncomfortable but once we found that the arrangements worked well, there came a great sense of freedom.

The most memorable parts of the trip were: Calcutta with its magnificent decaying Victorian architecture, a city full of cultural events and the heartbreaking poverty of its street people; Varanasi, a place of age old spirituality, with its ghats on the Ganges where elaborate prayers, and round the clock cremations took place; Pondicherry, a peaceful resort by the sea with its unique blend of Indian and French culture; and finally the long drive from Chennai on the east coast to Cochin on the west coast, through the paradisiacal state of Kerala, a vast tract of palms, temples and gentle people. We ended our tour in Mumbai.

After two days of exploring Mumbai we arrived at Fakr-ud-deen's shop, near the school. The area outside the school reminded me of the older part of Mombasa, near the port, the neighbourhood where Najma had grown up. Most of the homes here were low-rise blocks of chawls, one-bedroom flats, often twenty per floor, which housed large families. To me they seemed like modern caves, shelters for sleeping and eating. How did people live in such close quarters, and preserve any sense of privacy? The streets, on the other hand, were more like meeting places. Their open-air markets felt like theatres teeming with traders, shoppers, beggars, wanderers, and all manner of people, who had bit parts to play, with simple, often monosyllabic dialogue—aao, jaao, hato, betho—come in, go away, move aside, sit down. For emphasis, Indians always seem to repeat the words; an invitation to come in is always aao, aao.

The school lay at the end of a long narrow lot. On the left side there was a small administrative building, a basketball court and finally the school itself, a recently built, airy, seven floor building. Running along on the right was a wide path that ran all the way to the end. We soon discovered that the path was also used as a playground for the younger children, where groups of them came together to play ball or hopscotch or just mill around and chatter. Occasionally a scooter, or bicycle would sail through the path and the children would fly out of the way and then almost instantaneously reform their groups as if the disturbance had not occurred. It seemed that the children were adept at sharing the small space without much friction and were able to deal with disturbances without losing their concentration.

When I waited for Najma in schoolyards in Toronto where she taught, there were always teachers and assistants around, watching the children carefully and there was much pushing, shouting and shoving because, I realized later, there was the space to allow children to run around and be rambunctious.

The principal of the school, a woman in her thirties was energetic, well spoken, and professional. Her main interest was to have us teach English. The school curriculum was in English, but the children would revert to Hindi as soon as they left the classroom. The teachers spoke Hinglish. Our own accent is a mixture of colonial-era British, Kenyan, and Indian, with a hint of Canadian and some Swahili expressions thrown in unconsciously.

The principal wanted us to help the children develop an interest in reading for pleasure and listening to the English radio or any communication that would give them a better sense of the language, particularly the spoken version. We didn't need convincing; reading was the door that had opened up many worlds for us.

India has over four hundred languages, twenty-nine of which have more than a million native speakers. Indians from the South do resent, sometimes bitterly, the dominance of the Hindi-speaking northerners perhaps just as the Québécois resent the dominance of English in Canada. However, by and large, Indians speak Hindi and accept the need to learn English.

Until recently, the school had been partly funded by the local government. That had led to class sizes of sixty or more, and the quality of education had suffered and so the AKES had decided to privatize the school in order to reduce class sizes. In practical terms this meant parents would have to pay twelve hundred rupees a year instead of the fifty they'd paid under government funding.

We met some of the teachers we would be teaching with, and one of them, Chandrika, filled us in about the neighbourhood. It was not uncommon, she said, for a family of eight or ten to live in one room. Najma and I were no strangers to living in cramped quarters where privacy was almost unknown—but not in such deprived conditions. We had lived in small apartments but they were luxuriously spacious by comparison. I remember my family's first home, a single room that had two beds, a dining table, and a small sofa. We had a little kitchen that barely fitted three people, where we sometimes sat on wooden seats, legs folded, three inches from the cement floor, while my mother cooked chapattis and served them hot with a curry or two. The kitchen was in the common hallway and our own tiny bathroom had a pail that had to be filled up with hot water boiled in the kitchen before we could take a bath.

Najma's home was a three-bedroom flat of less than seven hundred square feet, in a colony not too dissimilar to the ones in Mumbai where Ismailis live. It had also been built about the same time, in the early fifties. It had been her mother who had saved enough money to put a down payment on a flat and move the family out of the old part of the city. She had taken in boarders to make ends meet and throughout her childhood, Najma slept in a room stuffed with bunk beds along with six other kids. Our lives were cramped and full of anxiety and fear, but the desperation of the people in the school's neighbourhood was far worse.

Chandrika gave us an example of the violence and abuse that takes place in the neighbourhood. When cell phones were first introduced, a young boy became fascinated with a phone that belonged to a teacher. He decided to steal it, but on the way home, lost his nerve, returned to the school, and hid the phone in a flowerpot. Eventually, the teacher found out who was responsible for the theft and confronted the culprit. He confessed and the school decided to have a quiet word with the family. The father, a very conservative Muslim, refused to meet with the female teachers, and the mother, who was expecting her seventh child, was terrified of the father. Finally, a *masi,* the mother's sister, accompanied the mother to the school and had a meeting with the teacher and the principal.

The mother refused to believe that her child was capable of theft. The father, she pointed out proudly, was an excellent disciplinarian. The boy was punished for any major infraction in one of two ways. He would be hung upside down and lashed with a rope. Or if the infraction was serious, he would be subjected to *mirchi ka dhuva*; his head was held down into smoke given off by burning red chillies. Najma tells me that in Mombasa, the local witch doctors would to try to exorcise evil spirits from those suspected of being possessed using this method.

The father did finally come around after much counseling and stopped subjecting his children to these medieval punishments.

****

That afternoon we went looking for the second school, walking up and down the street it was supposed to be on. Its entrance, with doors like a closed storefront, was lost in a busy and overcrowded sidewalk. We finally found it and entered through a doorway that immediately opened out into a large courtyard with a huge staircase leading upstairs. On the right side of the courtyard lay a small yard with two huge *peepuls*, or Bodhi trees, sacred to both Hindus and Buddhists. The principal, also probably in her thirties, met us and gave us a tour. The teachers, all female, looked at us curiously. The principal told us that about thirteen hundred girls attended the school in two sessions, with between fifty and sixty in a class. As soon as the lunch break bell rang, a flood of girls was released, little girls passing us on both sides, yelling or rushing at us and deftly avoiding us at the last minute. Later we found out that very few girls went beyond grade 10. They were sometimes trained to become hairdressers or seamstresses, while the parents kept an eye out for a suitable boy. Most parents did not consider it their final duty to make their daughters self-sufficient; it was rather to find a husband, a man from a good family with a well-paying job. The rest was up to Allah.

    We were given a quick tour. There was no air conditioning, the classrooms were small and the desks tiny, reasonably organized with pairs of desks in rows of ten or more separated by tiny aisles. The entire property probably took up half an acre.

    I thought back to our bungalow on Bayview Avenue in Toronto that sat on a quarter acre. With two kids, each with their own bedroom and bathroom, there was no room left for guests to be housed and there were too many books, perhaps a small library would have been nice. Sameena and Abid fought when they were young and the family room became a battlefield over the use of the TV or the music system or having their friends over. We sometimes toyed with the idea of moving up north to a bigger house but always reminded ourselves that we were living in a bigger place than we had dreamed of when we came to Canada.

Now I am glad they've both been to India for extended periods as adults. There are few better places to appreciate the preciousness of space, privacy and compromise than in the cities of India.

At the end of the tour the principal told us that being a male, I could not teach at the school but Najma was welcome. The two of us had a quick discussion about where to volunteer and decided that for reasons of coordinating transportation and our evening activities, it would be easier if we both taught at the first larger, co-ed school.

When we gave the principal of the bigger school our decision, she was delighted and introduced Najma to a teacher who was going to be away for a few days and they immediately started planning for Najma to take over her class.

Over the next few weeks we found out that most of the parents who were sending their children to the school could barely afford the fees but were convinced that education was the only escape from the grinding poverty that they lived in. The heads of families were taxi drivers, owners of small shops who sold basics like soap, and pop or spices, and perhaps got additional income from selling phone cards. Some worked as waiters at night and shop assistants during the day. A few were professionals. Some owned scooters. Many lived in a single room, sharing common toilets with neighbours. One of the biggest sources of income for many families was remittance sent by family members working as ex-pats or, in most cases, basically as indentured labourers for the many unscrupulous businesspeople in the Middle East.

Money also flowed in from Saudi Arabians to build *madrassas* for young Muslim boys to learn Urdu and the Koran. Many of those who could not afford to go to public schools ended up in *madrassas*. According to one report in *Asia Times* the Saudis want to promote "modern and liberal education with Islamic values" through the madrassas.

Even though education was expensive for the parents of children at our school, we discovered that it was inexpensive to take children to museums and parks or to Marine Drive for an outing. The Indian government has made it very affordable for local families to go to museums and historic sites, and the number of local people at cultural venues surprised us. In Canada, these places are, by comparison, the purview of the well off and cultured.

Most of the teachers belonged to the fabled Indian middle class. Some commuted for two hours each way. They were paid roughly 15,000 to 20,000 rupees (less than $500 a month), a good salary in India. Many have relatives in the West or in the Middle East, and one of the teachers, Rukhsana, was about to join her husband in Dubai. She was happy to have Najma's help as she prepared for the move. But she was worried about giving up her job because the papers were full of stories about Indians getting fired or fleeing from the hyperactive Dubai real-estate market, which was suffering badly from a recession.

11. In and around Byculla.

While Najma chatted to Rukhsana, I left the school feeling thirsty and found a small shop across the scooter filled street with a sign for Orange Fanta.

I noticed a small, dark elderly man with thick glasses, wearing a Gandhi cap sitting on a bench nearby. I ordered a Fanta and sat down at a table by the side of the kiosk. The man in the Gandhi cap came over to me.

"My name is Jagjit," he said. "You are going to volunteer at the school. I hear you are from Canada. Welcome to our neighbourhood."

The surprise on my face showed as I blurted out, "How do you know all this?"

"I believe in Lord Hanuman," he said with an impish smile. "He reveals all to me."

I said nothing and smiled back uncomfortably.

He chuckled and said, "I was only teasing you. The *chapprassi* told me everything. I know everything that goes on in the school. I am its oldest student, honorary student, that is."

"Honorary student?"

"I've been living in this area since the school opened in 1948."

I still kept quiet, trying to hide my skepticism.

He laughed. "I see you are puzzled. Let me tell you my story."

"I came here in 1948. I was eight years old. We come from Bihar. After Gandhiji was assassinated, my father used to say there was no one left to champion the poor and lower castes. It would be better to go to Mumbai. In a big city, people ask fewer questions about your background. In a village they know you are an *achoot*. They won't even come near us let alone touch us."

"So you never told anybody about your background?"

"They found out soon enough, but it was better than being in the village. We chose to work in this area because the Ismailis were building a colony, including a school, and we thought we would get a little shop outside the colony and sell sugar, salt, sweets and soda for the children and things like that. The Ismailis did not care about our *jaati*. Many of you are converted from the lower castes yourself. Many came from Gujarat and Kutch to escape the mayhem of the Partition. So many people lost their homes, even family members, in that madness."

"But weren't there problems in Mumbai?"

"There were, but the Ismailis kept guards outside and bribed some of the Hindu gang leaders to keep away."

"So the school was opened in 1948?" I asked.

"Yes, the original school was built in 1948. It was a boys' school for Ismailis only, and the Prince Ali Khan Hospital was built next to it in 1955, I think, and then in 2005, the foundation stone for the new school was laid."

"By the Princess Zahra?"

"Yes, by the princess, such a beautiful woman. She is divorced now, isn't she? Do you think she will succeed her father?"

"I would like that, but many other Muslims would be very offended. As it is, many Muslims don't consider us real Muslims. Having a woman as the head of our sect would be unacceptable, don't you think?"

"Well, we Hindus have a lot of goddesses," he replied. "Our goddess of knowledge, Saraswati, is, as you probably know, female. But I know some Muslims have strong feelings about the subject. In any case, I've seen all four generations of the old Aga Khan's family. First it was the old Aga Khan who had donated the money from the Diamond Jubilee in 1945. He came here to open this colony. Then it was his son Prince Aly Khan who came to open the hospital inside the colony in 1955. Then, in 1957, after the old Aga died, his grandson Karim Shah came here as the new Imam. I still wonder why the old Aga bypassed his son. And then Karim Shah's daughter Princess Zahra came in 2005."

The Diamond Jubilee was the fiftieth anniversary of the previous Aga Khan's ascension to the throne of Imamat. The Ismailis weighed him in diamonds, the proceeds of which he donated to build schools and hospitals and housing colonies for the Ismailis.

"So what did you mean by becoming an honorary student?"

"Well, I could not afford to go to school, and in any case, this school was for Ismailis back then, though now the majority are non-Ismailis. But I made a lot of friends, and one boy, Amir Lalji, gave me books and helped me to learn. He still stays in the colony. His father paid one of the masters to teach me for three summers. I learned to read and write."

Jagjit continued, "I am glad I learned to read and write enough to keep my books and read letters and so on but I never wanted to do anything else but run the business. Now finally I have sold the shop but I work keeping books for small businesses like this one."

"So all the caste problems are not a bother to you?"

"In the village it is still there. Less, but still there."

"But now it's not permitted to use the word *Harijan*, right?"

"Now they call us *Dalits*. Also Scheduled Caste, I don't even understand what that means. It is not our names that they need to change but what they feel in their hearts. Perhaps it will take generations for that to change, perhaps never. Still, things have improved. Jobs and places in university are reserved for us but there are always people who oppose that, like the Shiv Sena."

"I thought they only went after Muslims."

"No, no. They want everyone who is not a Maharashtran to leave Mumbai."

"You never think of going to a quieter place? Mumbai has become very crowded."

"No, no. Mumbai is home as far as I'm concerned. I have many good friends in Mumbai. They still drop by. Now Amir is retired, but we still go for tea once or twice a week at Iqbal's restaurant next door when he's in Mumbai. He often visits his son, who has gone to England. My son is also grown up and lives here. He works with these computers, bumputer or whatever they call it. He makes good money."

"You are not thinking of retirement?"

The man's shoulders shake with laughter.

"Arrey Sahib, retirement is a foreign *ka* idea. It's for those with money, the *paisawallahs*. We poor people just pray that Bhagwan keeps our arms and legs working till the last breath. If I stop working, what would I do anyway? I get up at four, do my *kirtan* before God, some yoga and start working at seven till four o'clock. I take vacations when the schoolchildren are off. I walk the streets of Mumbai then to see how much things have changed over the last sixty years. This is my life, and I don't want to retire. Nawaz, Amir's son, tells me retirement is big business in England."

"What does Nawaz do in England?"

137

"Owns old people's homes, these retired people you talk about. He has become very rich. Owns many homes and even hotels. Nawaz still comes to see his father every Christmas with his family. Always brings a gift for me. You are an Ismaili, from Canada, yes?"

"Yes, my name is Mehboob."

"Nice name. Means 'beloved' in Urdu, doesn't it. So what do you do, Mehboob Sa'ab?"

"I also work with computers."

"Where did you study it?"

"In Africa and then England."

"Did you go to Aga Khan schools in Africa?"

"No, to government schools, but Najma, my wife, went to one. She also taught at an Aga Khan school in Nairobi. As a matter of fact, we both went to college with Aga Khan scholarships."

"So you have come here to repay your *karz?*"

"Yes, I suppose that's why we're here, to repay our debt. Without those scholarships, we would probably not have got our education."

He smiled and looked across the street.

"There. Your wife is coming out of the school. Please drop by when you can, I am often here."

I waved Najma over and introduced her to Jagjit.

"Would you like a drink, Behen?" he asked.

Najma declined and we said our goodbyes.

****

Najma looked at the entrance of the Ismaili colony behind the little shop and suggested we take a look.

A guard dressed in khaki uniform raised his hand in a slow salute and motioned us in. The crowds, heat and hooting receded as we walked along a long, cool, clean driveway, lined with palms and almost deserted. We noticed a small park to the right and a large apartment block in front of us. Its windows were covered in a variety of brightly coloured and patterned curtains and a small garden full of roses and marigolds near the entrance gave the otherwise solid and spartan block a homey air.

Ismaili housing colonies often have a mosque and sometimes a dispensary run by a nurse or a school on their grounds, and they still exist in many cities of India, Pakistan, and East Africa.

"It looks really well maintained doesn't it?," I said.

"In a colony, everybody pays their bills. You never want it to be known that you don't pay your bills," Najma replied.

The colonies in Africa and India were all built in the 1940s and 1950s, and they had the same sort of functional architecture, even the same pale yellow paint, at least the ones I've seen.

I glanced at Najma and thought how different we are, as our friends often say, and yet we've stayed married happily for the most part. I recalled the first time I entered Makupa Colony, when Najma took me to visit her parents.

****

Jasmine and rose bushes surrounded the entrance to her home. The delicate scents outside were overwhelmed by the smell of curries and pilaf as soon as I stepped into the tiny flat. The foyer-cum-dining-room's cement floor was polished red, the dining table was pushed against the wall, and her father was sitting in his favourite armchair at one end, and in the tiny alcove at the other end stood a fridge that her mother had saved for years to buy. From the foyer area there were three entrances to small bedrooms and one to the galley kitchen.

This was the room she'd told me about, where she'd sat as a little girl, and listened to All India Radio, on a tiny Blaupunkt radio and learned to appreciate classical music, and helped her father complete the bills of lading he'd brought home from his office, where she had become captivated by names like Mumbai, Hong Kong, Vladivostok, and Amsterdam.

Her father's dreams of travel and art and music remained dreams, but he passed these on to Najma to fulfill.

She has started painting modern abstract works in oil now that she finally has a studio to create her own works. She has also built a library of Indian classical music on her iPod, a collection whose size and richness would have been unimaginable in her father's time, and to which she listens while she paints, walks or does work around the house. She has taken her iPod when we've travelled through China, a South American cruise and on trains in Europe.

The first night I was there, I stood till Najma's father asked me to sit down. I had difficulty in imagining him as a young man playing with Najma, teaching her to sketch or play the harmonium and talking about faraway places. He now looked remarkably like my father, short with wide shoulders and a potbelly.

Kulsumbai, her mother, came out of the kitchen, greeted me warmly, and excused herself to finish her cooking. Shamshubhai's words were welcoming, but his looks were wary. There were reasons for his guardedness. I was the first man Najma had brought home, I was seven years older than she was, and perhaps most importantly, he had heard from his sister, Malekbai, that I was not a suitable boy.

If you are an Ismaili, regardless of how little you are involved in the community, someone can put together a dossier on you and is quite willing to share it freely, especially if a marriage or business venture is in the offing. This information collection is now faster and transcontinental, courtesy of the Internet. Two things matter the most when a marriage is being contemplated: the piety and prosperity of the family one belongs to. It would be known whether your family was *dharmi (very religious), sara* (decent, middling folk), *thik* (okay), or *nastik* (nonbelievers) and whether the family ran their own business, were professionals, or working class. Malekbai was the drama queen of the family. As soon as Najma gave her my name, her extensive network produced considerable feedback, some spiced up, I'm sure. Najma confided in me that Malekbai had expressed horror at the way a *dayee chokri*, a sweet girl, like Najma had fallen for an obvious *goonda* from Nairobi, whose residents were known to be generally uppity and impious. I had long hair, a Fu Manchu moustache, and a Beatles haircut. My background check had revealed that the family was dubiously okay, the redeeming feature being my nanima, who gave generously to good community causes.

A year or so before, Malekbai had found a suitor, a clean-cut, observant young man, a daily mosque-goer, who was quite keen on Najma. To humour her parents and aunt, Najma had gone on a date with him. He had spent the entire time talking about his plans to expand the business and throwing out a lot of hints about his and his family's expectations of a wife and daughter-in-law. I suppose by contrast, my sharing of Najma's passion for Victorian literature and Indian music stood me in good stead.

Shamshubhai gave me a long, unblinking look, and after an uncomfortable silence, growled, "Would you like a beer?" He had a deep voice and was reputedly one of the best *Ginan* singers at the mosque. *Ginans* are hymns written about five hundred years ago by the Persian Pirs, who had intricately woven together references to prophets of Islam, Hindu gods, and beliefs in reincarnation to create a new faith, one that preached equality among all its followers. They probably drew large numbers of converts from the disadvantaged castes.

My mouth was dry and I was grateful that beer, frowned upon by the observant, was something Shamshubhai enjoyed. I looked at Najma, who was already smiling and walking to the fridge. Soon snacks, plates of hot kebabs, fritters, and samosas accompanied by green chili, tamarind, coconut, and other chutneys began arriving from the kitchen. Shamshubhai offered me *pili pili ho ho*—jalapeños—which I politely turned down, knowing the little devils would play havoc with my stomach but he chewed them as if they were peanuts.

Najma's mother had done her homework well. Her network, in addition to Malekbai had traced relatives, cousins, and second cousins (or cousin brothers as Indians like to call them) of my parents. She asked after each one and knew more than I did about what was going on in their lives.

Though she suffered from severe diabetes, she volunteered for three or four hours daily in the colony. She went to the homes of the old ladies to inject fellow sufferers with insulin or to leave them an extra portion of the food she had cooked or simply to share a cup of tea and some juicy gossip.

When someone passed away, they called Kulsumbai, longest-serving member of the *gusul* committee, first. She helped to clean and anoint the dead, swathed them in white sheets, and after the ceremonies, while the men went to bury the body, she and other volunteers helped the bereaved family cook a simple meal, of *kedgeree* and *daal,* for the neighbours, friends and family to eat at the wake.

After we had consumed a huge dinner and three large Tuskers each, I sensed Shamshubhai warming up to me. He offered me whiskey and looked very disappointed when I turned it down.

"No jalapeños and now no whiskey. A little too careful, aren't we?" he said, somewhat acerbically.

He then offered me a *paan,* betel nut leaves filled with a concoction of condiments to suit one's taste; various seeds, nuts, cardamom, shredded coconut. He made up one of his specials, not the sweet variety I'm used to but a very *khara paan,* a caustic one.

"The sweet *paans* are for women," he pronounced.

Not only did he proceed to make me a *khaara paan* but also added a wad of tobacco to it.

I chewed on the paan slowly and within minutes began to experience vertigo. I held onto the table and finally, Najma, realizing I needed to lie down, offered to show me books in her room.

Lying on the bed, I knew I had lost his respect. It was three strikes, turning down the hot jalapeños, the whiskey and now and I could not handle a *paan* with tobacco.

It was only after Abid was born that I think I regained his respect. If I could sire a son, I was a *mard,* a real man. He had never forgiven Kuslumbai for not giving him a son. Through seven pregnancies she had lost four male children due to complications from diabetes. Three girls had survived.

****

While we wanted our wedding to be a simple affair, Najma's parents insisted that it was unthinkable for their eldest daughter not to have a traditional marriage. The first ceremonial function was for the two fathers to negotiate a *mohr,* a sum of money to be paid by the groom to the bride in the event of a divorce, according to Muslim tradition. The groom's father always tries to beat the price down, and the bride's father tries to get the best possible deal. After consuming a bottle of whiskey, the two men settled on an acceptable amount. They were both proud, embittered by poverty, and now resigned to working as clerks to make a living. They had become dissolute, drank heavily, ate hot, spicy food, and were quick to feel slighted or angry when they sensed disrespect.

Najma's mother borrowed money and held a reception catered by herself and her friends. I remember Kulsumbai saying, "How can I face my friends and tell them there is no reception for my eldest." My mother was too ill to help at the time.

Though Ismailis from India have happily undergone conversion, they still maintain many age-old Hindu traditions. The day after our marriage, Najma had a *vidayi* lunch, a traditional Hindu ceremony to bid a tearful farewell to the bride. Custom conflicted with my preference when it came to deciding how Najma should address me. Kulsumbai's opinion was that Najma should address me as *"tamae"* (a respectful and formal way of addressing one's betters, elders, and husbands) as opposed to *"tu,"* the familiar form used between two equals. I had to assure Kulsumbai that I preferred being addressed as *"tu"* by Najma. I asked Najma's mother not to address me as *"tamae,"* but she ignored me to the end.

Women like Kulsumbai had desperately wanted their daughters to be educated. When the Imams exhorted the Ismailis to educate these women and treat them as equal to men, the women embraced education with enthusiasm yet generally their male counterparts were far less enthusiastic about the idea of educated equals. Marriages were still arranged affairs, and the men, of course, preferred compliant women. In our mothers' generation, the institution of marriage was often a terrible struggle between the sexes. The men often beat the women and my father was no exception.

It was my mother's plight that made me painfully aware of how oppressed women of her generation were. Only when I went to college and met Najma did I realize that things were really changing. But Kulsumbai knew that her life was not going to change: her greatest achievement was that her girls were educated, although not as much as she wanted. She just prayed that the husbands would treat them well.

Najma's was the first generation that went to college, pursued professional careers, dressed as they pleased, and dated men who were, for the most part, not afraid of educated women.

****

The sun was beginning to lower itself in the sky and the mosque at the colony was stirring with preparations for the arrival of the congregation.

" This reminds me so much of the mosque in Makupa. I'd like to go in for the dua. Do you mind coming in?" Najma asked me.

"Sure, it'll be interesting to see how the service compares to the ones in Kenya, " I replied.

But just outside the entrance, she stopped and watched people go in. The old women were dressed in long frocks with *pachedis* on their heads, carrying food offerings, and the younger women were all modestly dressed. I could smell the incense wafting out, and hear the strains of the old Gujarati *ginans*.

Seeing that she was hesitating, I asked, " Why are we standing out here?"

" I don't think we can go in."

" Why not?'"

" Look at the women. Not one of them is wearing pants."

" Does it matter? They'll know you are an outsider. Girls even wear jeans in Toronto. It can't be that different here."

" This is a different place. It's like the old days in Kenya- it was considered disrespectful to wear pants. I don't think I can go in. We'll go back, walk by the sea and I'll say my dua while we walking. Afterwards we can find a restaurant near Marine drive where they serve beer."

" You're going to say your prayers while walking?"

" Nowhere does it say that to pray one has to be sitting in a mosque. You can help by staying quiet while we walk, " she said laughing.

The next morning we took a taxi to the YMCA. The further we moved inland, the denser the city became, and the area around the central railway station was filled with a mass of humanity, shops, carts, cows, and cars busy trying, and miraculously managing, to avoid collisions. I imagined every bare square inch of the ground was being continually pounded and reduced to fine dust. When the taxi stopped, I looked out with relief. The YMCA, a compact, six-storey, modern-looking building inside a pristinely clean, walled compound had a small, meticulously kept garden fragrant with jasmine and frangipani. A tranquil island two blocks away from the storm surrounding the railway station.

We left our luggage in the room and went out to explore the neighbourhood and find some food. Next to the Y was a rambling, abandoned-looking Victorian mansion, also with a pretty garden and two huge ancient trees. Behind the mansion was a four-storey, brown-brick apartment with long bay windows, and where we could see inside, we noticed well-furnished rooms, with chandeliers, potted plants, and large, framed pictures. The Y, the mansion, and the apartments occupied one large block, an island of calm bordered by four busy roads.

On one side of this miraculous oasis lay an old *masjid* with a magnificent minaret and a sizeable complex that housed a *madrassa*. Judging by the group of young male students in traditional Muslim caps milling around, it must have been a large school. Behind the Y was a large collection of huts, a slum where women sat on the sidewalk watching children play. On the third side was a large open *maidan* where two separate groups of boys were playing cricket. In front of the YMCA were little old bungalows used for business and an office block that seemed to house a non-profit organization, a Christian missionary office, an Islamic religious books wholesaler, and a couple of medical offices. On the road between the Y and the businesses was a busy taxi stand, surrounded mostly by men with beards or turbans, trying to catch our eye.

A strange jumble of abodes, this would be our neighbourhood for the next month or so.

VI. TEACHING AND EXPLORING

"' Bambai to sone ki chidya hai,' a Muslim man in the Jogeshwari slum, whose brother was shot dead by the police in the riots, tells me. A golden songbird; try to catch it if you can. It flies quick and sly, and you'll have to work hard and brave many perils to catch it, but once it's in your hand, a fabulous fortune will open up for you......"

"The slums and sidewalks of Bombay are filled with little lives, unnoticed in the throng. But to each of them, the scale they are living in is mythic. It involves battles of good versus evil, survival or death, love and desolation, and the ceaseless life-affirming pursuit of the Golden Songbird."

Maximum City: Bombay Lost and Found by Suketu Mehta

12. Boys and Books.

Najma and I went out for an early dinner on Sunday, planning to rise early to start volunteering the next day. The friendly waiter asked if we were going to the Shivratri Festival that night.

"Shivratri? Isn't that an all night celebration?"

"Yes *sahib,* people celebrate all night and sleep late the next day."

"So the next day is a holiday—for everyone, even schools?"

"Oh, yes, Sahib. All schools are closed."

We had not been told that our first day at school was a holiday.

Legend has it that at a time when humans were threatened by an environment that had become toxic, the lesser gods approached Lord Shiva to inhale the poison that was destroying life on earth. When the power of the poison started to turn him blue, he wrapped a snake around his neck as an antidote and hence all the depictions of the dark Shiva show a snake around his neck. Shivratri, the night of the Lord Shiva was a celebration of the saving of mankind.

We went back to the Y and started to plan our next day, looking up places to explore. As I flicked through the TV channels, I realized that the Academy Awards from Los Angeles on Sunday night would be shown next morning in Mumbai. We hadn't missed watching the Oscars in years.

I got up at six and kept the volume low so Najma could sleep a little longer. When she got up we ordered tea and we settled down to watch the Oscars.

The Indian TV show hosts were focused on *Slumdog Millionaire.* The prizes started to roll in: Best

Picture, Best Direction for Danny Boyle, Best Original Song (A. R. Rahman and Gulzaar for "Jai Ho"), Best Original Score (A. R. Rahman) and four other Oscars.

    The Indians went wild. I was particularly delighted for A. R. Rahman, whose music and career I have followed for years. I first heard Rahman's music in the film *Bombay*. In some ways the film was your archetypical song-and-dance-filled Bollywood extravaganza and yet it addressed one of India's most serious issues since Partition; religious prejudice. A modern day Romeo and Juliet tale in which Shekhar, a Hindu journalism student, and Shaila, a beautiful, shy Muslim woman fall in love. Despite opposition from their parents they escape from the seaside village where they were raised and settle down in Mumbai. The couple and their young children get caught in the brutal Hindu/Muslim riots in their neighbourhood, an episode based on the murderous events that we escaped by mere days in the early part of 93.

    The music, created by Rahman, is a unique fusion of Indian and Western music with overlays of mesmerizing Sufi hymns. Several groups protested against the film including the Shiv Sena, because it portrayed them as instigators of the murders, and the orthodox Muslims, who protested the lifting of the Muslim heroine's veil by her Hindu lover. Some theatres showing the film were forcibly closed. The film went on to win several international awards.

****

    Rahman's own life story is incredible. He lost his father, also a musician, at the age of nine and became the primary breadwinner of the family. With gigs most nights and practice sessions during the day, he was finally forced to drop out of school in grade 11. He worked mostly with older, struggling artists who made him realize that he had to, as he put it, "look beyond what you are forbidden to look beyond." He began experimenting and one of his early commercial successes was a jingle written for the

Indian mobile provider Airtel, one of the most downloaded pieces of music in India, with 60 million hits.

Rahman was born a Hindu and named Dilip Kumar. "After his family went through trying times,'" according to the *Times of India,* Rahman and his mother and three sisters converted to Islam, in fact, to Sufism. His art is inspired by facets of Sufism such as the dance of whirling dervishes of Turkey and the Sufi poetry of the saints of North India.

Syed Kareemullah Khadari, the Pir who converted Rahman, gave him a new name, Allah Rakha—One who is taken care of by Allah. To this day, if he is in Chennai on a Friday, the musician worships at the Hazrat Dastagir Durgah, where Khadari is buried. Whenever he buys a new instrument, he takes it to the Durgah to be blessed. He also took his Oscar statue to the mausoleum to be laid at the foot of his master's grave, part of the Sufi practice of respecting and honouring one's teacher.

The Oscar winning Best Song of that year, "Jai Ho," - Let There Be Victory, is written by the Indian poet and filmmaker Gulzaar, a Sikh, also comes from an impoverished family and worked as a car mechanic before becoming a writer, musician and one of the most popular poets in India. He has a mesmerizing voice and is a legend in his own lifetime.

I often wonder how men from such humble beginnings succeed in a society where competition is fierce for whatever is left after nepotism and corruption swallows its share of opportunities.

****

After the Oscars, Najma suggested we explore the neighbourhood. We found a Coffee Day, India's "Starbucks", about a ten-minute walk from the Y. After our coffees we headed to a restaurant next door for lunch: Shambu's Restaurant Pure Veg (as opposed to impure veg?). We downed a couple of chunky and tasty *parathas,* with *raita* (spiced-up yogourt) and two teas. That cost, a dollar fifty. For dessert, we picked up six cookies from the bakery next door. Price: fifty cents.

We walked back through side streets, stopping to look at a small glass display cabinet containing a cheap-looking statue of Christ with two bulbs, one red and one yellow, over his head. The case had been nailed to a large bodhi tree, under which a scruffy-looking man sat praying. Beside him, there was a big sign saying, "Good luck to all taking their ICSE or HSC", the final exam for college entrance.

Within fifty or so yards, a few street women were napping while their children were playing with little mounds of debris. A row of tenements, all six storeys high, then took over. I was a little taken aback by the goats tied at the entrances until I remembered that the festival of Eid was around the corner. I guessed these creatures would soon be slaughtered in celebration of Ibrahim's sacrifice of his son, Ismail (Abraham's son, Isaac, in the Old Testament).

These grimy chawls reminded me of the tenement in Nairobi where my mother and I lived for a few years. Our building was painted gray, but unlike the chawls, it had sidewalks, dusty and messy, but clear of garbage. There were other stark differences between our tenement and this one. These chawls had four times as many flats on each floor and each had probably three times the number of people living in them. And unlike our neighbours, this population was entirely Muslim and poverty-stricken.

Though they were filthy, we didn't feel threatened near the slums, on the streets, or in the markets. People either ignored or smiled at us but never appeared menacing.

As we passed the tenements and came close to the Y, a group of raucous boys hanging around the *paan* shop, smoking and spitting out the betel nut juice stopped to look at us. I became a little wary but as we passed, they made way, recognizing us as foreigners and politely saying, "Hi, uncle, Hi, aunty."

****

The next day we got up early, had a large breakfast, and looked for a cab to take us to the Aga Khan school. It took a while before we found a taxi driver who knew where the school was. There is no simple street address system in India. We had to explain that it was the school after the railway bridge near the St. Mary's school.

The streets were filled with scooters, tuk-tuks and cabs, and the occasional cart pulled by a cow, while the sidewalks were crowded with pedestrians, street vendors, and beggars. Over time we noticed that scooters often carried two children, invariably without helmets, and the cabs were frequently shared by groups of people, who were dropped off individually along the way.

I could not help but notice that the schoolchildren, whether in downtown Mumbai or in the inner city, always looked freshly washed, had their hair combed, and were dressed in neatly pressed uniforms.

As we made our slow progress along the narrow street, it seemed that sitting in our taxi, removed from the action, we were watching a compelling documentary.

The slum right behind the Y was waking up, and from one corner of it, we noticed half a dozen men emerge, walking out in single file. They were blind, and those who had more sight were leading those who had none. A little further on, we saw a group of women in black burquas chatting and dawdling along. Behind them was a girl in jeans listening to an iPod, trying to bypass them. In front of our cab was a small but shiny new BMW. A beggar walking with a staff suddenly dashed out onto the street and started knocking furiously on its closed, tinted window. The driver of the car ignored the man with the badly disfigured face.

As we turned a corner, my eye fixed on a tall, beautiful young woman standing on the curb. She was perhaps in her twenties, engrossed in combing her long, light brown hair that hung below her waist. She looked freshly bathed and was wearing a bright white *salwar* and a flowery blue tunic. Questions streamed through my mind. Where did she bathe? Was that her family, huddled under the blankets next to her? Was she going to work, perhaps in a call centre? Who protected her?

A few yards further was a makeshift stand serving *pao bhaji,* perhaps the most popular Mumbai sandwich. The *pao* is mini-bread filled with *bhaji*, a potato-based vegetable curry garnished with onions and coriander.

The cab dropped us off across the street from the school. We stood for a few moments, watching the chaos at the school entrance. Finding an opening in the traffic, we dashed across the road, vying with the mass of scooters, taxis, and mothers walking their children into school.

By now quite frazzled, we managed to enter the school and find the vice-principal's office. Amazingly, everything inside was running normally, and the maelstrom outside seemed inconsequential. The VP escorted us to the staff room and introduced us to four young women teachers who would help us settle into the school.

****

We sat through those teachers' classes all morning. Most of the learning was done by rote, but as always in India, there was a surprise.

Advanced computer technology had been professionally and enthusiastically adopted. There was a network of PCs with overheads in each class, and the teachers and students were quite comfortable with digital slides, videos, and Word documents, among other computerized aids. In this respect, the school was far ahead of the ones in Toronto where Najma had taught. The biggest challenge facing the school and its teachers was the English language. Everything is taught in English; it's the language that most Indian parents want their children to learn but the parents don't speak it at home and it's not the language of the schoolyard, the streets, or television.

The children were learning the rules of grammar and basic reading and writing as mechanical skills without appreciating the power and beauty of the language. Their singsong expression was laboured. In addition to teaching in a foreign language, the teachers were driven by one objective —to get the children to pass their exams. Results were all that mattered.

Having brought up two children, we appreciate the immense energy and time needed to foster curiosity, independent thought and an interest in reading. These skills were not even a consideration for most of the parents in Byculla, often uneducated and simply battling for survival, and for whom grades were the only measure that mattered. Only the most academically gifted would rise to the top and receive higher education. I remember a shocking statistic; overall in India less than 7% students graduate from high school.

By lunchtime, we realized that there were very few Ismaili students or teachers left in the school. The neighbourhood, we were told, was predominantly Muslim, and much of the Ismaili community, for whom the school was originally opened seventy years ago, had either moved out to the northern parts of Mumbai such as Bandra and Navi Mumbai or emigrated to England, the USA or Canada.

****

The next day Najma found her niche.

Like the sensible and practical person she is, she offered reading classes to various teachers. I watched Najma teach a full class of students in the afternoon and realized that class discipline was not going to be easy.

I decided to take on two kids who needed remedial help and spend the rest of the time with my writing and business projects.

"Will we make a difference?" I asked philosophically.

"Just do it," she replied testily.

By the end of the day, we'd done the quintessentially Indian thing—carving out a place for ourselves amid chaos.

The two children I took on were around nine, and both had been held back because of their inability to pass grade 1. My job was to teach the boys frequently used words, to try to get them to construct sentences, to read to them, and to encourage them to talk and give them some confidence.

Najma and I were shocked by the social Darwinism that prevailed in the school. In grade 5, where she was teaching, all children who didn't get 40% were failed and held back. It is a brutal society to live in.

Farhad, the older boy, was about ten, good looking and gangly with straight hair that fell over his forehead. His ears stuck out of his black hair in a way that reminded me of myself at that age. He looked sad, but I managed to get a shy smile from him when I joked in Hindi. His classroom teacher told me that he was the first in his family to go to school and that it was at the insistence of his twenty- one-year-old brother. His father did not care about his school education and, like many poor Indian fathers, wanted him to get a job as soon as possible.

Akhtar, a nine-year-old, appeared to be a more sanguine character, a plump little bespectacled fellow with very short hair. He was shy, inspected me carefully, and betrayed no emotion. Clearly he was trying to size me up and I guessed he would make a good poker player. He had two siblings, and his father worked in a youth hostel. He didn't know as what. His classroom teacher told me that since he was the only son, the family treasured and coddled him.

I began by asking each of them, "Tell me about your family."

Apart from Mummy, Daddy, and siblings, out came Dada-Dadi and Nana-Nani (paternal and maternal grandparents) and a host of uncles and aunts (chacha-chachi, mama-mami). I could sense who their favourites were by now.

Farhad clearly worshipped his brother Sharik, a taxi driver who had a cell phone. And he became animated and smiled as he talked about his nanima. She liked green *dupattas* (scarves) and made wonderful *biriyani*. I remembered my nanima, who loved a deep blue *pachedi* with delicate silver and gold embroidery. It covered her round head and the tight, tiny bun.

For Akhtar, the only son, Daddy was the hero. Daddy took him everywhere on his scooter.

Clearly the extended family was the centre of their existence. Though I was curious, I refrained from asking them about where they lived. As a child when I lived on Grogan road, I was always embarrassed to be asked where I lived. In Mumbai only 25 percent of families live in apartments, and over 75 percent reside in slums or *chawls*. It struck me that that none of these children, poor by western standards, had a beaten-down look to them. In fact they appeared clean, lively and polite, nobody had told them they were disadvantaged. Poverty, in the Indian context is about survival, whereas in the west it is about the quality of life.

Their descriptions reminded me of my own extended maternal family: my nanima, my favourite uncle, Amir mama, and all the *masis*. Often in times of difficulty, and there were many, it was the extended family that provided the support needed to carry on. There was no other safety net.

The boys shook their heads when I asked them if they had any books at home or any favourites. I was fervently hoping to lead them to some sort of interest in reading by the time I left.

I visited the school library to look for books that might be interesting and suitable for Akhtar and Farhad. The books for this age group were ancient and alien to their Indian readers, about children in England who played in their backyards or kept pets. Keeping pets, particularly in this neighbourhood where there is barely enough room for the family to fit into the usual one-room household, is unknown. There were few if any backyards in this area.

I chatted with the librarian, who was acutely aware of the issue with books and told me that new ones had been ordered but it would take time. She told me that few children read at home and warned me in particular, not to give the children books to take home because their parents would make them memorize the tomes. Books were viewed only as necessities for passing exams. "Remember," she pointed out, "India is a land with an oral culture, where grandparents pass on the myths and fables. Even music that has existed for hundreds of years is yet to be written down."

"I suppose the television fits in comfortably with this tradition of oral folklore," I said.

"Oh, yes," she replied. "Look at how popular *The Mahabharata* series is on TV, it has been running for twenty years."

Obviously, no new books would be arriving while Najma and I were at the school, so I decided to buy a few books for the two boys from some decent bookstores in the city.

Over the next two days and the weekend, we went on a mission to buy books for Farhad andAkhtar, and tickets for concerts and plays for ourselves.

Our first stop, the Crossword bookshop, was in the middle of upscale Kemp's Corner, full of restaurants, high-end designer stores, gyms and other establishments catering to the needs of the affluent. Its most famous landmark, a multi-storied home being built for the richest Indian, Mukesh Ambani, stood on a hill guarded by security men who shooed us away. When finished, it would supposedly become the most expensive personal residence in the world, projected to cost over $1b dollars.

Sitting at the entrance of the bookshop, playing with a mound of fine dust, were two children; a girl, perhaps five years old, dressed in a dirty torn dress, and a boy, about two, naked from the waist down. They were immersed in building ditches and cones or just letting the dust trickle down from their tiny fists.

I watched them for a minute or so. Everyone else walked by; I realized that given time, I too, would have to become oblivious to their plight.

Inside, I combed through the children's section. There were only two mothers looking for books with their children. I found few books with an Indian background, and the ones that I thought might be interesting seemed to be poorly written. I consulted Najma, and she helped me select *Franklin Plays the Game* for Farhad and *Berenstain Bears* for Akhtar. Franklin was about a boy who liked everything about soccer: the colour of the uniforms, the playing fields, and so on, but he couldn't get the ball to do what he wanted it to. *Berenstain Bears* was about a family of bears: Papa Bear, the woodworker father; Mama Bear, homemaker and part-time businesswoman; and their three children, Brother Bear, Sister Bear, and Honey Bear. The stories were modern and based on family problems solved with the advice of father and mother.

Our decisions made, we had a coffee and bought some cookies at Moshe's, a nice little Western-style café inside the bookshop.

When we emerged into the heat and noise of the street, the little girl playing in the dirt rushed forward and held out her hand. I sat down on my haunches and tried to chat in Hindi.

"What do they call you?"

Pointing to the boy, she said, "Pappu," and then, pointing to herself, "Priti."

They were shy and giggly. Beneath her mask of dirt, Priti had a beautiful face with large eyes and fine light brown hair. Round-faced Pappu had a runny nose. They didn't seem malnourished and appeared to be quite content to sit and play in the dust for hours.

"Where do you live?"

Priti pointed to the flyover, a huge bridge, next to the bookshop.

"You mean under it?"

She smiled without answering the question. I gave them most of the cookies I'd just bought. I would have liked to find a way to wash their hands before they ate them, but they happily gobbled up the goodies and went back to playing.

I looked around, wondering if someone was watching them, a handler who controlled them or the parents. There was no one except the bookshop guard who looked at me disapprovingly.

Our next stop was the Oxford bookstore and it was the same story there: not many books for the boys' age group and only two families with children looking for books. The two largest bookstores of a city with probably half the population of Canada with no more than a handful of parents did not make sense.

Did Indians not encourage their children to read because as the librarian at the school pointed out, this was a country that still relied on oral knowledge? It seemed to have skipped the written word and embraced films, television programming and computer technology.

We decided to do more book-hunting the next day, this time on the streets.

It was Saturday morning, and I slept in while Najma went for her usual morning walk. We met up in the dining room, and as she started to tell me what had happened during her walk, a middle-aged English woman, Katherine, asked if she could join us.

Najma had stopped for a cup of tea from a street vendor, a chaiwallah, when she noticed two elderly women sleeping not far from his cart. The two women got up and called out to a little boy who was sitting nearby. One of the women took off three bangles from her wrist and gave them to the boy. He walked over to the chaiwallah, and handed over the bangles, without saying a word, and was given three cups of tea, one for him and two for the women. When Najma was given her specially prepared cup (without sugar), the vendor, sensing Najma's curiosity, told her what was going on. The women, who made their living selling bangles on the street, often pawned the bangles until they had the cash to redeem them. They were residents of the area, set up shop in the same spot near the vendor's cart and slept there every night.

When Najma finished her account, Katherine wondered out loud where the women bathed themselves. Najma and I had often asked ourselves the same question about people who lived on the streets. We found one answer during a morning walk in Calcutta. We noticed a small family—a man, his wife, and a young girl—stop at a construction site on the main thoroughfare of the city, Mother Theresa Sarani. The girl and the man held a saree as a large screen, behind which the woman apparently undressed, passing her clothes to the man. Feeling like voyeurs, we walked on, and on our way back, we noticed the woman looking fresh and bathed, holding one end of the saree while the daughter took a bath. Later we discovered that there was a water hose on the site, which the family used on the sly when the workers were absent.

Katherine had her own story from a walk she'd taken that morning. She described how a lame man led four blind men from the colony behind us across the busy road in front of the railway station. How cars slowed down to let the procession slowly walk across and how amazing it was that disabled people helped each other.

Katherine told us about her exploration of Mumbai. She travelled by train in the zenana compartments and struck up conversations with women who would talk to her. She added that since she was unaccompanied, she would often get stared at in the general cars "even though I'm no longer a young bit of fluff."

Discovering that we were volunteering and we were Muslims, she asked Najma why she wasn't wearing a hijab. When we laughed, she was relieved that we weren't offended. Najma patiently explained that Islam, like Christianity, is divided into many groups and that in the Ismaili sect, particularly in the west, wearing a hijab is not a common practice.

Later I asked Najma why she bothered to explain, she said, "I am a teacher, and if someone asks, I give him or her the facts."

After breakfast, we picked up a cab outside the Y and were dropped off not far from Churchgate.

The Victorian and Edwardian facades in the Fort area of Mumbai were drenched in brilliant sunlight. This part of the "great ruined metropolis," as Salman Rushdie calls the city where he was born, looked glorious under its blue sky, perhaps because the Saturday morning crowds were thin, more relaxed and quieter.

The wide sidewalks, the buildings and the warmth of the sun reminded me of a downtown neighbourhood in Nairobi dominated by a thoroughfare called Lord Delamere Avenue. It was built in the early 1900s, with two- or three-storied solid grey edifices, a bit of Edwardian England in Africa, standing on a wide boulevard full of palms, small hedges, and tall eucalypti. The sunlight would fill the huge windows of the stores that sold an eclectic mixture of safari tents, guns, flowers and books. And there was the landmark outdoor café at the New Stanley, where Hemingway wrote under the thorn tree.

Nairobi has suffered the same fate as Mumbai from encroaching modernity. Villagers have poured in, cars have multiplied, the air has thickened, and slums have mushroomed. The downtown core, filled with similar colonial architecture, has lost its sense of spaciousness and solidity. Lord Delamere Avenue has now been renamed Jomo Kenyatta Avenue, and the area is as crowded as the busiest parts of Mumbai. Nairobi, too, has become another great ruined metropolis.

People are afraid to walk in many areas during the daytime, and nobody walks at night. We don't go to Nairobi much now. There is as much a fear of crime as there is of destroying wonderful memories: the carefree strolls in the evenings, going to the cinema, and afterwards going to eat kebabs or sitting in the car till late listening to our favourite songs.

But in Mumbai, for all its ills, we have always felt completely safe.

We started our walk at St. Thomas's Church in front of Horniman Circle and ambled towards the Strand Bookstall, a landmark in Mumbai. It turned out to be a wonderful little store on two floors and stuffed with books. We were looking for a book for Abid, and we leisurely flipped through a number of thick volumes. I couldn't resist buying a book called *India: A Sense of Place,* and when we went to pay, we were invited to sit down by the manager. When complimented on the selection, he replied that he just didn't have enough space to create enough sections, so things were somewhat topsy-turvy. But if we ever wanted something, the clerks could find it. Najma immediately asked for *India* by Raghurai, the subcontinent's foremost black and white photographer.

She purchased the book for Abid. Having bought an excessive number of outfits for Sameena, she'd been worrying about finding something substantial that would please our son, and now she was satisfied.

We noticed a picture draped with a little marigold garland. When I asked whose picture it was, the manager told us that it was the owner, Sham Bagh, a book-loving legend in the city, who'd opened the shop to promote the love of reading, always at discounted prices. He had passed away just days before.

We walked out and went south towards the sea. As we went along towards the magnificent Victoria terminus, I stumbled upon a street stall, an Indian surprise, full of books that were ideal for Farhad and Akhtar. I recalled that thousands of books were sold on the streets of Calcutta in the same way. And now I began to notice many stalls in this area of Mumbai, often tucked away on side streets and corners. With no respect for copyright laws, the government allows ridiculously cheap copies of Western and Indian bestsellers to be sold on sidewalks. This is the most popular, and affordable option for Indians and perhaps explains the absence of parents in conventional bookstores.

Najma and I picked up *Winnie-the-Pooh, Tom and Jerry*, and eight other similar second-hand books. The vendor, a healthy bare-footed young man in torn jeans, Rajesh helped us choose the books, cautioning against any that would be too advanced or not interesting for my students.

"Are you in college?" I asked.

"No, I left in grade 10 and came to Mumbai."

I remembered reading somewhere that half the total population of India is between the ages of 15 and 25.

"Where did you come from?"

"Delhi, Sa'ab."

"Why come here?" I couldn't resist asking.

"Too much tensun in the family."

The memories seemed to pain him.

As I handed him over 300 rupees a wide grin appeared on his face. I was probably the best customer he was going to get that day. For less than eight dollars, I'd acquired a treasure that could help Farhad and Akhtar start their journey as readers.

Najma, needing to do her own shopping, left me to explore the area on my own and we decided to meet back at the Y. As Rajesh packed the books, I noticed a group of young men sitting on their haunches, on the sidewalk perhaps ten or so yards away from the bookstall. Some wore old-fashioned turbans on their heads.

"Who are these people?" I asked him.

"Just came into the city today, from the villages mostly. They have no one to receive them," he said.

Noticing a disparaging note in his voice, I asked, "What do you think of these new people?"

"Well, how many can this city contain? They come prepared to work for anything. They keep our wages down and there is no room for these people to even sleep. They dream of getting rich and becoming fillum stars. They are stupid," he said a little angrily.

I smiled. It was the same old story, older immigrants railing against the newer ones. I took one more look at the group of newcomers and wondered where they would spend their first night.

As I watched the seemingly hapless immigrants from the countryside, I guessed that most of them carried with them great dreams and drive. Some would find success in unbelievable, wonderful ways; others would live and die on the streets

I walked around the group of newcomers in search of something to eat and decided to go for Mumbai's favourite snack, *Pao bhaji*.

"Twenty rupees," said the first street vendor I came across.

I gave him a hundred, and while he was getting change, he kept on reciting his musical sales mantra.
Pao Bhaji khao,
Sir, bees rupyeh,
Khao, arey Mister, Khao,
Pao Bhaji khao.
Eat bread and spicy veggies,
Only twenty rupees.
Eat, Mister, eat.
Eat bread and spicy veggies.

As I started to bite into my sandwich, I caught the eye of an elderly woman. She looked away and moved a little farther back. I looked at the vendor and asked:

"Kohn hai? Who is she?"

"Meena is a poor woman, not a beggar, and does not have enough money for food. She teaches some of the street children English."

"Can I buy her a *Pao Bhaji?*"

"Of course. She will give you many *duas*."

I took out another twenty and the vendor's assistant took the snack over to the woman.

Feeling a bit awkward, I started to turn away but she stopped me, thanked me, and added: "I don't ever beg but I am grateful."

"You do social work? Teach?"

"I just help a little. I have nothing to do. I was laid off a year ago and can't get a job now."

"What were you working as?"

"For twenty years, I worked as a cook in the company cafeteria and also looked after office supplies and did clerical work too. Now that the recession has hit, the work is gone. I can't feed myself."

"No pension from the company?"

"There is, but it pays for the rent and not enough for food. My story is a long and sorry tale."

"I can listen if you want to tell me."

She began slowly, speaking as if it were someone else's story.

"After my marriage, I could not conceive. My in-laws said I was barren and useless. I had brought in hardly any dowry. They persuaded Rohit, my husband, to take another wife. She, too, could not bear children. Finally, Rohit came back to me asking for forgiveness and begged me to take him back. By now, I had a job and became the main breadwinner, supporting him until he died of pneumonia after a long illness three years ago.

"I regret having no children," she continued, "but having children is no guarantee to happiness either. I had a friend who had signed over the proceeds of her husband's life insurance over to her son and daughter-in-law and was pushed out of the family home. Lives in an ashram for widows in the North, Kashi or some other holy city.

"Being a woman in India is *paap ki saza*, - punishment for misdeeds in a past life," she added bitterly.

I shook my head in sympathy, not quite knowing what to say. Perhaps realizing that I was distressed by her story, she brightened up and said, "I have much to be grateful to Ishver for."

"What would that be?"

"I have a roof over my head, and when I am really unhappy, there is a *mandir* very close to my house. I pray, I am sure Ishver listens and I feel at peace afterwards."

The lot of most Indian women who outlive their husbands is as terrible as was the fate of widows in Kenya decades ago.

****

I doubt if my mother would have named me Manu, a revered and learned sage, had she read some of the laws he laid down for all social classes of Hinduism. One that is still observed today goes thus.
"In childhood a female must be subject to her father, in youth to her husband, when her lord is dead to her sons; a woman must never be independent."

The story of Lilla behen, who rented a room near my nanima's house, has always stayed with me. A young woman in her thirties, she was left to look after her two children, Raju and Kamla, after her husband passed away. She became a seamstress. Although Raju was older than us, he played with our group of young boys. He was a big, gentle boy and had left school after grade 7. He had tremendous dignity, an oval face, straight, thick black hair, a shy smile, and sad eyes.

His uncles, who looked after Lilla behen and her family after the father died, gave him a job in their business of repairing and selling cars. They were not averse to receiving stolen cars or even stealing the occasional car and stripping parts from it. Raju was a great mechanic and did much of the physical work. One day, while working in their yard, he was caught in a police raid and the uncles let him take the fall. He was put into a correctional facility in Kabete on the outskirts of the city.

I remember going to visit him with his cousins on Sunday afternoons when he was allowed to receive visitors. He would sit with us on a grassy patch at the top of a small, windswept hill in front of the long, single-storey brick prison, chatting, eating potato chips, and drinking Coke and we always made sure that he got the biggest share.

One day, I was told that we would no longer go to see him.

"Why?" I asked a few times.

"Because Raju has died."

"How did he die?"

There was a long silence and Ranjan, his cousin, explained how Raju had committed suicide.

I was twelve; it was utterly shocking and incomprehensible that someone would lie down on the train tracks going from Nairobi to Naivasha to kill himself.

Ranjan finally said to me that it was understandable. Raju had killed himself rather than face the shame of his thirty-five-year-old mother having become pregnant after an affair with a neighbour.

"Even our good name has been destroyed," Ranjan said to me.

Name and honour were very big things, even among thieves.

I remember that Ranjan had once told me, "We were *chamars* in India, but now we are an upper *jaati*. Here we are car dealers, traders."

That was only one of many remarks made by my Hindu friends about caste. A Patel friend whose sister had fallen in love with another Patel had said to me, "I know the boy she likes is also a Patel, but he comes from the seven village group and we are from the ten village group. Unacceptable. My father is very upset."

I was always confounded, and still am, by how Indians have divided themselves into so many castes.

After Rajus' suicide, it was reported that Lilla behen also died during childbirth. Years later, my nanima told me that she had probably been murdered by her deceased husband's brothers.

Kamla, the remaining child, went to live with the uncles where she was underfed, abused, and beaten. She was a dark, bubbly girl with flashing eyes and two pigtails.

Henry, nanima's cook, liked her and gave her leftovers from nanima's kitchen. One day, she was discovered eating in Henry's room. She was dragged out howling and screaming before being severely thrashed. I remember her sitting under a large tree, black and blue with swollen lips, and not allowed to play with us for many days.

Ranjan told me that, like her mother, she was a rand, a whore, going to the room of a black man and taking food and who knows what. It was unforgivable.

A few months later, Kamla ran away. I never knew what happened to her.

Meena finished her *pao bahji*. I thrust two hundred rupees in her hand and walked away as she started to protest. For women like Meena, things have changed little in two thousand years.

13. Visits.

Farhad picked *Franklin Plays the Game* and Akhtar got *Berenstain Bears*. Somewhat to my surprise both the boys took to the books and could easily relate to what I thought were books written for western audiences.

I decided to hand out the other books slowly, one at a time, hoping that the families would get used to the idea of having books at home for pleasurable reading, not for studying.

I started to experiment with getting Farhad and Akhtar to start writing. Each began a simple journal on my laptop, four or five sentences a day.

Every day for an hour and a half with each boy I got in some reading, some writing, a chat, and exercises of making sentences from simple words and rhymes. The journals began to take shape.

After the boys left, Kirit, the peon who had been assigned to look after me, brought in a cup of tea. Embarrassed by this special attention, I told him there was no need for him to take the trouble but he totally ignored me. When I suggested he might put less sugar in the tea, he made an attempt to do so but he kept forgetting and so I tried acquiring a taste for milky, syrupy tea.

When I first heard the word *peon* used to describe Kirit, I was a little taken aback. In the West the word is a disparaging term, but in India it's a job. In a society where employment is an extremely valuable commodity, the position is even considered respectable. I always found myself impressed by the dignity and poise of the older peons, waiters and ushers, and the pride with which they performed their tasks. There were also several older women, sweepers in the school, who never let any dust or garbage accumulate, and kept the school spotless. They all seemed to be focused on their particular set of tasks and went about their jobs in a methodical, dedicated fashion. There was a calm acceptance of their place in the hierarchy, and I had the strong sense that they prized seniority above all else in their work.

One day, after I'd sent the boys home, Kirit and I sat down for a chat.

"How long have you worked here, Kiritbhai?"

"Ever since the school was built and for ten years in the old school before the Princess Zahra came to open this school. You are an Ismaili from Canada, Sa'ab?"

"Yes," I replied, "and where do you live?"

"Very close by, in a *jopadh patti*. It's a good colony."

"In what way?"

"We have water and electricity and even a small clinic, Sa'ab. Some slums have to buy even water from the *goondas*. The municipality collects garbage regularly. You know, in some colonies garbage is not collected for two, three weeks."

"So it's comfortable?"

"Always difficult. No space, six people in one room. My mother is still alive. There is always tensun. But I have work, a secure job. Many others don't."

"How many children?"

"Two boys and a girl of marriageable age. Looking for a suitable boy for her. . . . And you, sir?"

"A boy and a girl. She is still studying and he works."

"You people don' t have the dowry problem."

"No, we are fortunate." I didn't tell him that it costs me an arm and a leg to put Sameena through university abroad.

After Kirit left, I felt at a loose end.

Since Najma was going to teach till the lunch break, I decided to go for a little walk. As I passed by his store, Fakr-ud-deen rose up to greet me and remembered me as the thousand-rupee phone credit customer. When he discovered that I'd finished my teaching for the day, he insisted that I sit down to have tea with him. This time we got properly acquainted, the Indian way, by exchanging information about our families and jobs. He had a son Adnan, who had two children at the school: Rubina and Aftab. He was extremely proud of them and told me that they were in their tenth and eleventh grades and that he was very happy with the school.

His other son, Tayeb, worked in Dubai as an accountant for a construction company while his family, a wife and daughter, continued to live in the neighbourhood. Tayeb sent money home to Fakr-ud-deen as well as to his own family. With what his son sent from Dubai and with Adnan's help in the business, Fakr-ud-deen lived well. He also had a daughter, Lubina, who was a nurse.

"Lubina is unmarried," he added mournfully.

"Does Tayeb come home often to see the family?"

"At least twice a year. He is a professional, not like the *hathodiwallahs,* the men wielding the hammers and sledges, the common labourers."

"I hear they are treated badly," I said.

"Let me tell you, it' s terrible. These Arabs have no respect for the Indians. They are supposed to be our Muslim brothers but treat us like *janawars*, take the passports away and put ten or fifteen people in a room. They only respect the *goras*, just for having white skin. But what to do ? We need jobs."

He lowered his angry voice. "The Arabs even come here to take advantage of us. Some of the older men come here for a second or third wife, you know. They pick a young beautiful girl and take her back as a wife. Is that a marriage, I ask you? The parents are just selling the girl. It' s a sin."

"They come to this neighbourhood?"

"Yes, I have known of cases."

He saw the look on my face and added, "But they don't pick the girls from the school. Too educated for these *janawers*."

He sipped his tea and calmed himself.

"But let is talk of more pleasant things. Tell me how you got to Africa and Canada."

Just as I started, Najma entered the shop. We stopped talking and Fakr-ud-deen said, "Come in, come in, behen. Your husband and I were getting to know each other. Join us for tea."

"The peons told me you were here," she said addressing me.

She then turned to Fakr-ud-deen and said, "Thank you. We have to go for lunch at someone's place. Perhaps another time."

We had been invited for lunch by the parents of Abdul, a friend of mine in Toronto. He had asked me to take some gifts for them. Najma had phoned them the previous night, and they had insisted that we come for lunch. Najma tried to explain to them that we eat only light food at midday but they urged us to visit them all the same.

We headed to the nearby colony where Abdul's parents lived, the one that we had explored on the first day. The guard at the entrance of the colony hardly glanced at us.

"Where is Block H?"

"Straight on. Turn left and fourth block."

Some old men were sitting on benches outside the mosque, reading newspapers or chatting. Older women dressed in old fashioned frocks down to their ankles and *pachedis* draped around their shoulders were out and about, some talking with the neighbours, others bringing their grandchildren home from school for lunch.

One couple that was haggling with a vegetable vendor, reminded me of Najma's parents. They would have felt right at home here in Mumbai.

Najma's mother was a truly fearless woman. I recalled going shopping with her to a Mombasa slum where the Somalis had settled after one of their interminable civil wars. The refugees had taken over a large portion of the slum and often carried guns, which they were prone to use when serious arguments started. Most Indians stayed away from these areas for fear of being kidnapped or assaulted, but Kulsumbai went right in and argued for discounts with men who terrified me.

Najma stayed quiet as I searched for Block H. Eventually I was forced to turn to two women for help.

The younger one wore a frock and the older, a sari.

"Where does Zehrabai Somani live?"

"Block H, I think, isn't that right?" the younger woman asked the older one.

She nodded and turned to us.

"Where are you from?"

"Toronto, Canada."

"Really? I have a son in Mississ . . ."

"Mississauga?"

"Yes, that's it. His name is Alim Walji. Do you know him?"

"No, we live in another part of the city."

The younger woman chided her friend: "*Array . .. !* Do you know people who live on the other side of Bombay? How can these people, in a big American city, possibly know Alim?"

She then turned to us and asked, "How is Zehrabai related to you?"

"Not really our relation," I explained "but her son Abdul is a good friend."

"Ah, yes. Abdul. He is doing very well, isn't he? Did his accounting in England, no?"

We finally located Block H, and with some help, ended up on Zehrabai's doorstep.

She welcomed us with a large smile and warm embraces. Her husband, Mehdi, was watching an episode of *Mahabharata* on television and waved us in. Zehrabai was a short, heavyset woman with henna-dyed hair, a large nose ring and air of utter calm and control. Mehdibhai was a quiet little man with sad eyes.

Zehrabai invited Najma to come to the kitchen with her while she finished her cooking. Mehdibhai and I were given hot tea. We quietly watched the rest of the episode, one that I'd watched before. Just after Sameena was born, not wanting to leave her with babysitters, we watched the 94-part TV series *Mahabharata* not once, but twice. We would have to pause often so that Najma, with her prodigious memory, would help me work out the scores of familial relationships and the myriad subplots, backstabbing and intrigues and I could occasionally do some translations of the Hindi for her. It was by far the most complex story we'd ever tried to understand—a mixture of religion, mythology, philosophy and pure drama.

This TV series, produced by B.R. Chopra in the late 1980s, is one of the most watched TV programs ever broadcast in India.

Mehdibhai was watching the episode about the famous rigged gambling session, in which Yudister, the oldest of the five good Pandav brother loses his kingdom to the scheming Kauravs. Then, in the final bet, Yudister throws the loaded dice and loses his wife Dropati. The evil cousin Duriodhan, the eldest of the hundred Kaurav brothers, then tries to strip her naked in the open court. She prays for salvation, and Lord Krishna comes to her rescue and performs the miracle of elongating the cloth to the point that it was impossible to take it off.

Mouth-watering aromas wafted from the kitchen, and finally, *bateta champs* appear. A potato chop is minced beef in a mashed potato jacket fried in egg batter, delicious but deadly for the heart-disease-prone Indians. Each was served hot, off the wok, and impossible to refuse.

Najma then produced the two hundred dollars that Abdul had sent, along with a bottle of cologne for Zehrabai and a Johnny Walker Black Label for Mehdi bhai.

Mehdi bhai perked up at the sight of the whiskey and offered me a drink.

"It's too early for me," I said apologetically.

Zehrabai gave him a disapproving look and the bottle disappeared quickly. Zehrabai inquired about our children, our jobs, and the usual quick bio of our lives, while she tried to recall any connections with our surnames and places of origin. She was originally from Gujarat as well. We found out that the couple had eight children and many grandchildren.

The phone rang for Zehrabai.

"The girl is very pretty," she said to the caller. "Very bright and yes she's adopted. The parents are very *sadharan*. The girls from these ordinary families are well trained. She will make your son happy, of that I am sure... of course, there is no family wealth, but you will get many blessings from the Mowlana."

She put the phone down and grinned. "They want the girl," she told Mehdibhai.

He grunted, "Who else will marry that oaf? But he is good hearted and she is bright and beautiful."

She turned to us: "I do this *seva*, for the poor girls."

Zehrabai went on to tell us about the girls' hostel she visited twice a year and also raised funds for. Many of the girls were orphans or abandoned and therefore not desirable as wives. But having married off six daughters and two sons, Zehrabai was now somewhat of an expert at arranging marriages and helped out girls from poor families.

We said our thank yous and left.

14. Getting to know Farhad and Akhtar.

I held my lessons at one end of the spacious library, its many windows and floor of shiny tiles made it an airy sunny room. We sat at one end of the library on a long, low table, high enough for my long legs to fit in, opposite each other.

As I gained their trust, Akhtar and Farhad relaxed and started to tell me more about themselves and their families. Farhad's family lived in one room. His eyes lit up when he talked about Sharik, his twenty-one year-old taxi-driving brother, the one who'd insisted that he come to school.

Part of his education was for him to practise his English by describing his everyday life.

"What do you do on weekends, Farhad?"

"Sharik takes me to see nana and nanima every Sunday. They live far from here in Sakinaka. They make us *biriyani*."

"Is that your favourite food?"

"Yes, " he said brushing his hair aside, "I like *biriyani* very much, and sometimes nanima even makes samosas. If Sharik gets a lot of customers, he has extra money and we take bananas or oranges for them."

"What about Saturdays?"

His face turned serious.

"Daddy takes me for lessons at the *madrassa*."

"What do you learn?"

"Urdu and the Koran," he said shrugging his shoulders.

I slipped into Urdu. "Who is the teacher?"

"*Janabji* ".

Nobody in Canada would ever refer to a teacher as an Honoured person.

"And do you say the *Dhikr*?"

"Yes—*Allah u Akber, Al Humdulillah, Subhan Allah.*

He started to rock back and forth as he chanted the prayer-- God is great, All praise is to Allah, Glory be to Allah.

"How long do you go for?"

"Two hours. Daddy takes me and brings me back."

"What about films?"

His face lit up again and information poured out.

"I like Sharukh Khan, Hritik Roshan, and Abishek Bachan. I also liked Sanjay Dutt in the movie *Munnabhai MBBS*."

I noticed a lack of women in his list.

"What was the last film you saw?"

"Jhoda Akber."

Najma particularly detests Bollywood movies, but this was one that we both went to see. Most Bollywood offerings are song-filled, formulaic fantasies, and Jhoda Akber, somewhat unusual, was an entertaining historical romance.

The marriage of the Mogul king *Akber the Great* and the Hindu Rajput princess *Jhodabai* is one of the legendary stories of India. Most likely the fifteenth-century marriage was a shrewd move on the part of Akber to build an alliance with Rajput princes who opposed Muslim rule. The film was a highly romanticized version of Akber's pursuit of the princess. The handsome Bollywood superstar, Hritik Roshan plays Akber, and shows his rippling muscles and prowess with the sword in order to win the hand in marriage of Jodhabai, played by Aishwaria Rai, the Miss World of 1994.

"I liked the film too," I said to Farhad. "Who did you like best in it?"

"I like Hritek Roshan."

"What about Aishwaria Rai?"

"Yes, she's nice," Farhad replied in a polite, uninterested tone.

Farhad clearly lived in a simple man's world, not interested yet in the other half of humanity.

"What about television?"

"Yes, I like *Dhamal* a lot."

"Tell me what happens."

He described scenes from it in English, trying hard not to slip into Hindi. Animated fragments with nasty criminals chased by cops in jeeps, accidents as cars piled into a canyon, a jumble I had a hard time figuring out. As the words poured out, he reverted to Hindi, corrected himself and continued. It was the liveliest description he ever gave.

We'd established a bit of a bond by now, and I asked him to write everything he'd told me on my PC.

By now, Akhtar had also opened up quite a bit. His classroom teacher told me that he appeared a lot more confident and had begun to answer questions in class.

He'd brought in a book called *The Camel and the Evil People* that his Daddy had bought. It was about the Prophet's fight against a tribe that opposed him. "Peace be upon him" appeared at every mention of the Prophet's name.

I dutifully read it to him and later asked him which one he preferred: *The Berenstain Bears* or *The Camel and the Evil People*. I was relieved when he chose *Berenstain Bears*.

That day he had read particularly well and appeared unusually relaxed. After the class I casually asked him," What do you do on the weekends, Akhtar?"

"Papa takes me to the *masjid* and the *madrassa* and the aquarium sometimes."

"What do you do at the *masjid* and the *madrassa?*"

"At the *masjid*, I do the *wadhu* and wait for the *azaan* , and at the *madrassa,* I learn Urdu."

"You like the aquarium?"

"I like to see the fish swimming and the whale bone. I've asked Pappa to get me a small aquarium at home."

"What does he say?"

"Mummy says no. There is no place to put the fish tank."

"That's too bad."

I did not ask Akhtar to describe this home but I pictured him living in the kind of single room flat that Zul, a close friend of mine, had once described to me.

****

Zul had become well acquainted with an Ismaili couple that was having financial difficulties. They had invited him to dinner and he had been taken aback by the couple's struggle to co-exist in a tiny space with their three teenage children.

The flat, located in a five-storey building with ten apartments on each floor, was a long room, about twelve by twenty-five feet. One end of the room had been partitioned off to provide a small bedroom for the couple. At the other end of room, in two corners lay an improvised bathroom and a kitchen. A clothesline had been strung on the two walls of one corner, and a sari was hung on the cloth line when a family member took a bath. The triangular prism formed by the two walls and the hanging sari was just large enough to accommodate a pail of hot water and the bather. A towel was placed below the sari to prevent the water spilling into the room. The other corner, the family kitchen, housed a two plate electric stove and a small cabinet that contained kitchen utensils and basic food rations. A small dining table had been placed next to the 'bathroom.'

In the middle of the room lay three beds, two at right angle to the wall, one along the wall and a TV was installed on the opposite wall. During the day, thick handmade bedcovers and long roll pillows were placed on the beds converting this arrangement into a living space. At night this communal space became bedroom to their two daughters and son.

****

"Is there something other than an aquarium that you would like, Akhtar?" I asked.

"Yes. I want a laptop like yours. Daddy says if I pass class 7, with 60 then he will get me the laptop.

"Do you play sports? Cricket or football?"

"Sometimes, at school."

"And television?"

The face lit up. "I like cartoons very much, especially *Tom and Jerry.*"

I thought of Abid and Sameena. They each had their own laptop and access to the desktop in my home-office; a wireless modem in the house, high-speed connection, phones, and a cable TV with video on demand in a large, home-theatre.

Both Abid and Sameena as youngsters had persuaded me to purchase aquariums for them. Once the fish arrived, cleaning and shopping expeditions for their food were tackled with great gusto. But in a few weeks the shock of discovering dead fish, which had to be given a proper burial in the backyard, their enthusiasm disappeared. The aquariums, dry and empty, now lie somewhere in the basement.

They both liked the outdoors and loved playing in the backyard and both took up playing hockey and soccer.

Farhad and Akhtar had no place to play. Watching Bollywood films and television was their main form of entertainment and going to religious classes was a regular weekend affair. Playing cricket or soccer are mostly makeshift affairs played on little side-roads or school grounds.

India has made me look at space differently. a precious asset.

****

15. Terror attacks.

Throughout our stay in Mumbai, the papers were full of one story, the terror attack that had taken place on November 26, 2008, and which was referred to in India as 26/11. Ten distinct locations, including the Taj Hotel, the busy Victoria Terminus, and various restaurants including Leopold's had come under attack by a group of young Pakistani men who'd entered the city under cover of darkness, on a boat apparently from Karachi.

Only one terrorist, Kasab, had survived, and I followed his trial for many weeks.

The most interesting coverage was a transcript of his police interviews published by the Times of India. I had to work hard to decipher the Hindi/Urdu transliteration but I think I got a realistic sense of what the young man was like. Other papers and the TV gave their own versions of Kasab's personality which, of course, were much more sensational.

From the police interview it appeared that Kasab was an ill educated, poorly spoken and often confused young man.

He came from an impoverished family, the son of a street vendor in the town of Faridkot in Punjab, Pakistan. He seemed to have led an aimless, and for the most part, unemployed life till early 2007. Encouraged by his father, he accepted a job working for a mullah and was soon sent to a training camp reportedly run by Lasker-e-Taiba, a terrorist organization whose aim was to "liberate" Muslims living in Indian administered Kashmir.

The man who was mostly portrayed as a tough, murderous terrorist, seemed from the police transcripts to be an illiterate, hapless young teenager who had somehow been brainwashed into committing this terrible act.

One day, after my classes were finished, I went shopping in the vicinity of the school. Within five minutes of walking in the intense heat, I broke out into a sweat and decided to take refuge at Fakr-ud-deen's shop.

Tea appeared as soon as I sat down.

"You always carry this back pack. What do you carry in it?" he asked.

"My computer, which I use to teach and write, and the *Times of India,* which I read everyday."

"I do that every day too. You must be reading about the terrorists. The world has gone mad." Fakr-ud-deen sipped his tea loudly.

"The papers are saying that the Pakistani government is involved, that the ISI, their secret service, is mixed up in this business."

"I wouldn't be surprised at all if these ISI goondas are involved," Fakr-ud-deen replied with a shrug.

"Why do you say that?"

"It is the job of these secret service *wallahs* to create problems. When things are quiet, they let off a cracker and start these kinds of problems, to make themselves more important and employed. You don't think these CIA and FBI wallahs aren't doing the same?"

"Perhaps you are right, but aren't you concerned that this can start a war between the two countries."

"I don't think that will happen. Manmohan Singh is a peaceful man, but if it was that Advani leading the country now, it could be a problem. I'm more concerned about the troubles here in Mumbai. These days I hear grumbling about how we Muslims are still a problem for India. There are always *goondas* who want to start troubles so they can loot and rape."

"Like they did in '93?"

"Yes, those were terrible times," Fakr-ud-deen replied quietly.

"I read about what happened in the papers. Fortunately for us, we left just before the serious troubles started."

"When did you leave?"

"We left on the 2nd of January '93."

"You remember the date? You have a good memory."

"Were you affected by the riots?" I asked him.

Fakr-ud-deen remained silent for a few moments.

"Yes," he replied slowly in a far away voice. "I remember those days. I will never forget."

Then he started talking in a very subdued voice.

"We were living a mile or so from here on a quiet street. When the riots started, all the Muslims bought provisions—food and water and such like—and stayed indoors. I used to watch from behind the curtains to see what was going on outside on the streets. One day, the neighbours across the street came out. They could have run out of rations or needed to go to the doctor or something. Nafeesa and Hakim were in their thirties, nice, quiet people. I wanted to call out and tell them to stay off the streets, but they walked so fast and before I could get out to call them, they were gone.

"They got back in half an hour and when they tried to enter their home, they were surrounded by these *goondas,* probably the Seniks of the Shiv Sena. Some of the Hindu neighbours acted as lookouts and must have phoned the *goondas* to tell them about Nafeesa and Hakim coming out of their house.

"The *goondas* started to pour petrol on him. She got down on her knees and begged and begged.

"They stopped and told her to go inside.

"One by one they went in, and took their turn with her. They would come out sometimes zipping their pants, laughing and slapping each other on their backs.

"When they were finished, Hakim was screaming at them. They laughed and poured more petrol on him and struck a match.

"It's terrible to see a man run and writhe on the sidewalk."

"I could not bear the sight, I still feel sick when the memories come back".

He paused and continued, "The next day we buried him.

Nafeesa stayed in her room for the mourning period of forty days. My wife and the women in the muhallah took care of her and the children. There was always someone with her during that time. We were afraid she would commit suicide. She wanted nothing to be reported. In any case, who would have taken action? So many people were being killed and we knew the police were turning a blind eye to these atrocities- sometimes even talking part in the crimes."

Fakr-ud-deen stopped for a few moments.
"But then we had our *badla* ."
"We?"
"We, the Muslims. Dawoodbhai's boys came to our rescue and took revenge."
"Dawood, the gangster?"

At the time, Dawood headed the most powerful Muslim crime syndicate in Mumbai with the innocuous name of Company D, an empire of drugs, smuggling, prostitution, and many other illicit activities.

"He may be a gangster, but he restored our honour," Fakr-ud-Deen said angrily and then continued. "Dawood's men came and recruited the boys whose mothers and sisters had been raped, whose fathers and brothers had been killed by the Sena."

"In March '93, they bombed Mumbai: tirteen, imagine tirteen, locations bombed in one day: The Stock Exchange, the Air India building, the Sena headquarters.

"Halavi ditha bhenchodo ne, durre che havey—we shook the sister fuckers and now they are afraid of us."

Fakr-ud-deen's voice was shaking and spit was flowing out of his mouth. He wiped his mouth and took a sip of his tea, calmed down, and continued to speak.

"After things quietened, we moved to this street where now almost everybody is a Muslim. That's what has happened to Mumbai after the riots. Hindus and Muslims live in separate areas. It's a lot safer. I see Nafeesa sometimes. She has worked hard and put her children through school. They are in college now."

Fakr-ud-deen became quiet, a customer came in, and I slipped out.

****

After my chat with Fakr-ud-deen, I did some research. I uncovered a world that was almost beyond belief.

The bombing of Mumbai (which also killed many Muslims) created a rift between Dawood and his Hindu lieutenant, Chhota Rajan. Dawood is now considered to be part of Al-Qaeda and is currently believed to be living somewhere in Africa, after being forced out of both Dubai and Pakistan under pressure from the Indians and the Americans. Chhota Rajan reportedly moves between Kenya and the Far East.

The war between these two is legendary and many attempts at assassinations have continued over the past decade, adding another dimension to the divide between Hindus and Muslims. For a while he moved his residence to Dubai but continued his business activities in India, the ship-breaking industry in India and using it for smuggling in arms, explosives and contraband into the country and reputedly also in the control of the 'hawala' system. The word hawala meaning "in trust" in Hindi is an informal money-transfer system used primarily by individuals to transfer cash, locally or overseas, to people who do not have access to a bank.

****

That weekend we went to South Mumbai for a long walk on the promenade along the sea, part of the walk my father must have taken before he left the subcontinent.

Three months after the terror attack on Mumbai, we could still see clear signs of the destruction. South Mumbai is the historic part of the city, full of grand old Victorian, Gothic and Art Deco architecture. Not too far from the Taj Hotel are the buildings in which the East India Company set up its headquarters and ruled the country for two hundred years. Nearby, in the opposite direction, is Mani Bhavan, where Gandhi spent time thinking through and planning his strategy of *satyagrah* or 'truth-force' - nonviolence—to remove the British from India.

It seemed to me that the terror attack was part of the terrible, unhealed wound left by the Partition of 1947. The separation has created bitter enmity between people of the same race who essentially speak the same languages, share the same music, poetry, and food, and much of the same cultural values.

We stopped near the Gateway of India and stared up at the Taj. I tried to imagine the fear of the people inside the majestic hotel as the terrorists spread through the various floors, killing workers and looking for guests. Camera crews stationed outside witnessed the destruction of the now boarded-up old wing of the hotel and filmed images that were rapidly transmitted around the world.

We walked slowly past the destroyed part of the hotel where we'd stayed in 1993 and the heavily guarded entrance, where guests were lining up to go through a checkpoint and decided to continue on towards our favourite old haunt: Leopold's, the café where we often relaxed and ate our meals during our first trip.

Despite the terrorist attack on the cafe, it was full. The waiter asked us to wait for fifteen minutes but came back in five. He must have recognized us as foreigners, beckoned us ahead of the locals in the line, and asked us to share a table with a thin, elderly, Italian woman named Carlotta. She knew some Hindi and practised it on us.

She worked in the fashion industry, had a retail and wholesale business in Milan, and had been born in Ethiopia. She spent a few months in India every year. After she sent her designs to suppliers in Mumbai and Indore she travelled to India to oversee the production of, I imagined, expensive and fashionable dresses.

The talk turned to the recent terror attack. Leopold's had come under fire because it was always filled with foreigners, high-value targets for the terrorists.

The waiter who seated us joined in the conversation and pointed out the three entrances, two on Colaba Causeway and a smaller entrance on the side street, from which the terrorists had entered the place and opened fire. He said he'd ducked under a table to escape the bullets and splintering mirrors. I looked around, wondering what it would have been like to be trapped in here with bullets flying and suddenly I felt cold and claustrophobic.

Still full of anger, he said, "These *kasaii*—butchers—murdered ten people: two waiters and eight customers. One of the waiters was my friend. I held him in my arms after the attackers ran away, the cowards."

Seeing our discomfort, he said, "The foreigners have just started coming back, so we are pleased to see you."

I thought of my own experiences with terrorism.

****

One dark night my father came home, his shirt covered with blood. My terrified mother took his shirt off and cleaned him while I, seven at the time, lay listening to him tell her what had happened.

It was Wednesday, the night he always played gin rummy at the club. It was his friend Hassanbhai's turn to drive the car, and he'd dropped off Karimbhai, another regular partner, along the way.

My father remained seated in the back instead of getting out to sit in the front. When Hassanbhai stopped at a red light, the front door was yanked open and a man forced his way into the front seat.

Brandishing a knife, he barked, "*Towa paisa.*"

As the shakenHassanbhai fumbled to get his wallet, the man continued, "*Yenyu wahindi ni kama maalaya ya musungu*—you Indians are like the prostitutes of the whites."

Before he realized there was someone in the back, my father, a strong, compact man with a fierce temper, had encircled the robber's neck with his right arm. In the ensuing struggle, Hassanbhai suffered most of the cuts, but the assailant dropped his knife and escaped. With Hassan bhai bleeding by his side, my father drove the car to the hospital.

Fortunately his cuts were superficial and Hassanbhai recovered quickly.

From that day onwards, my father locked all the doors and windows of his car no matter where he was going. The doors and windows of our home also began to remain closed at all times.

Even today, an open door at home makes me uncomfortable. The sliding door that led out of the house to our backyard was always a particular concern to me since our children left it open often. After a summer barbeque in the backyard, when the children were younger, I would walk around before bed-time making sure that all the doors and windows at the ground level of the house were locked while, behind my back, the children would be making signs at each other -- "Here we go, crazy old dad."

But perhaps the worst terrorist encounter I've ever had was an incident outside my nanima's house.

My parents were out for the weekend and had left me with my grandparents. At around seven in the evening, I was sitting on my nanima's bed as she recited the prayers.

Suddenly, we heard shots in the air followed by shouts. She finished the prayers quickly, put on her slippers, and rushed out, instructing me to stay put. My grandfather, more careful, peeked out from behind the curtains after he'd tried in vain to stop her.

I could see neighbours armed with field hockey sticks milling around outside.

After the police arrived, nanima returned and told us that the Sikh family next door had fired shots in the air and had rushed out with hockey sticks when they'd heard screams in the small valley behind the houses.

They'd scared off the men who were attacking their sixteen year old son, Tari, a great hockey player. I worshipped him.

"Tari has been hurt badly," she told me after coming in and added, "Don't you ever stay out after the curfew, do you hear?"

The next day she told me that Tari had died.

Much later, I found out that his throat had been slit and his body hacked, the kind of killing the Mau Mau carried out to terrorize the Indians and Europeans. Now whenever I see a tall, young handsome Sikh boy, I think of Tari.

Then there was the tale of Chanda, a girl who had been kidnapped for ransom in Nairobi. A friend pointed her out to me and told me her story when I was about ten. She was very thin, and the skin on her face was covered with dark splotches. Her eyes were wide, and her mouth was slightly open, her buckteeth showing. Her mother was guiding her along.

She had been found buried up to her neck, with her head above the ground, after she was kidnapped and was rescued two days later. She never talked clearly after that, just babbled unintelligibly.

Several years later, I saw her with her mother again. She had grown much taller and looked like a scarecrow dressed in a nice frock. Her eyes were still wide open and her mouth slightly open. Her body was flat and thin with no sign of any curves.

16. Tales of Extended Families.

I was grateful for the TV in our room at the YMCA. Being an insomniac, I often stayed up late and watched soaps after Najma had gone to bed. Perhaps my predilection for watching the occasional Bollywood soap stems from my quintessentially Indian childhood in Kenya: a joint family with Nanima ruling the roost, arranged marriages, daughters-in-law who had to toe the line, servants, the desirability of fair skin, the Hindu-Muslim divide, and the pervasive caste system. What I see in Bollywood soaps is what I saw in daily life in Kenya, less conservative, to be sure, but echoed in the lives of many Indian families in Nairobi

To this day many Indians love this kind of family drama soap. It provides a powerful insight into ancient cultural forces at work in modern India. The relationship between mother-in-law and daughters-in-law, still drives some of the most powerful and emotional interactions in the family. Brides who who join the family but bring in inadequate dowries are sometimes murdered with the involvement of the mother-in-law. There are special jails for mothers-in-laws who are convicted of these crimes.

By comparision my own nanima's interactions with her daughters-in-law were pretty tame and often hilarious.

She had nicknames for all her daughters-in-law, whom she mocked to a greater or lesser extent, depending on their individual recent behaviours. None of them were good enough for her sons, though my youngest uncle's wife was the most favoured. She was called "The Doll." The oldest daughter-in-law was "Tiny," and the middle one was "Fajli," daughter of Mr. Fazal, whom she especially disliked.

I found Mr. Fazal fascinating. A large man with a booming voice and thick spectacles, he always called me by my Hindu name, Manu, whenever we visited his home. He would also invite me to pray with him in his *mandir*, a room that had been especially set aside for worship. Dressed in his singlet and a *dhoti,* he would light the incense sticks, and with hands folded, he would recite *slokas* from the *Geeta,* praying in a sonorous voice to Laxmi, the goddess of wealth. He proclaimed his Hindu beliefs and practices openly, even though he was a Muslim. No one seemed to find this particularly unusual. I felt quite at home in his little *mandir,* and there were always nice snacks after the prayer. His daughter, Shirin bai, was very much the modern Ismaili woman, dressed in short skirts (just below her knees), and calling my uncle "darling," which made the rest of the family snicker behind her back. She was buxom, had short, black, wavy hair, and was very fair, the looks that made Nurdeen, my middle uncle, agree to the arranged marriage.

After the marriage, she made him accompany her to the mosque every Friday. We all knew that he went because he had a roving eye and enjoyed looking at pretty women and flirting if he got an opportunity. I suspect he often flirted to get a rise out of Shirinbai, knowing that it made her jealous. Nurdeen mama always had a twinkle in his eye and produced a large guffaw when he was amused. He started balding early in life, a matter that bothered him immensely. All the lotions and herbal remedies he purchased had no effect, but he kept on trying. He was fond of reading *News of the World,* and I vividly remember the first time he gave me the paper and said, "I think you're ready to read this. You don't have to hide and read it, but just don't tell anyone I gave it to you."

Of course, *News of the World* had little to do with global affairs. The edition he gave me had a full-page picture of Diana Dors, his favourite actress/model, displaying her ample bosom. It also had a particularly sexually charged story of a landlord who was murdered by his lodger after he'd found out that the lodger had been having an affair not only with his wife but also with his eighteen-year-old daughter. I could not reconcile the people I read about in the *News of the World* with the English people I had encounters with; proper and reserved people who talked in clipped tones. They seemed so unlike the newspaper's murderers, rapists, bigamists, embezzlers, and other unsavoury but interesting characters.

Shirinbai loved to go shopping but there was the one car that was to be shared by all the women of the family and nanima insisted that she needed the car every morning at ten. This caused friction, even fights, but nanima was unbeatable. Ever since I could remember, she would go to visit my uncle Sultan who had been institutionalized at the Mathare Mental hospital. I was told that a blind midwife had bungled his birth and left him with a severe speech defect. In those days, he was called *gando,* a mad man. She would sit on her bed with her *tasbi* in her hand, praying every day that Uncle Sultan would miraculously become normal. He was a giant of a man, extremely gentle most of the time but could unpredictably fly into violent rages. The hospital, on the outskirts of the city, was a long, single-storied, series of brick buildings with red tiles and barred windows that looked like a low-security prison and I would often accompany nanima to visit him in this frightening place.

The warden Mr Sharma was especially fascinating, in an evil sort of a way. He regularly reminded us that he was a Brahmin, as if to say he did this work out of some higher purpose. A tall, dark man with straight, oiled hair, he gave the impression of being a man to be reckoned with. I suspect that Nanima disliked him, but she was always nice to him, bringing presents at Diwali, and praising his wonderful work for the inmates. Mr Sharma would allow me to peek into the yard when the inmates were let out. Many sunned themselves stark naked. He laughed when I shrank back.

Nanima depended on Benson, the driver, to help with the shopping after these visits were over. One day, during the Mau Mau uprising, Benson came back with a tale that took my respect for Nanima to even greater heights. Benson, tall and slightly hunched, was a quiet, dignified man of few words but on this occasion he could not stop talking about what had happened outside the Kariokor Market. That day, Nanima was tired and had instructed Benson to go and get chickens from the market. Mutua would slaughter the live chickens at home usually. Whenever I was there, if a chicken was being killed, I would watch, both fascinated and repulsed, as the neck was wrung and then slit. Sometimes the bleeding and headless chicken would run around the yard before it collapsed and became still.

At any rate, that day in the market, Benson was choosing young, plump chickens when he heard a commotion and came out to see a man struggling against the side of Nanima's Vauxhall. As he got closer, he realized that nanima was holding one of his arms inside the car and would not let go. Apparently, the man had approached the car and knocked on the window. Nanima had opened the window enough to talk to him, whereupon he had stuck a gun into the opening and asked her to hand over her purse. While seeming to reach for it, she had grabbed the man's wrist and yanked his arm into the car, making him drop the gun and hit the side of his face into the top of the car. Nanima had screamed and yelled at the robber until Benson came out. Then, with the help of the amused bystanders, Benson captured the thief and handed him over to the police.

    Mutua, the oldest servant of the household and Benson were part of the family and probably knew more about what was going on with individual family members than anyone else. They took sides and had their favourites. Benson always sided with Nanima in keeping the car under her control. Mutua would cook what his favourite children liked, and my Uncle Amir was first on his list. I remember Mutua shaking his head when the quarrels within the family turned into fights. Both Benson and Mutua stayed in service with us for decades. When Mutua became old and began to forget my name, he called me Mtoto ya Daulu—child of Daulu. After Mutua died, Nani who had always hired house servants from the Wakamba tribe because she knew the language hired a young Luo named Henry. He had ink-black skin, small shiny eyes, and a brilliant white, toothy smile. He was built like a middleweight boxer and always wore checked shirts and long, khaki pants. Nani would sit in the kitchen on a stool and chop the coriander or onions and teach him to cook curries and *kejdee*. Henry loved cooking and would experiment, but often with mixed results. Sometimes, after an unsuccessful experiment, Nani would shake her fist and call him "*haramzaada.*" Even though this meant *"bastard,"* she always said the word softly, with laughing eyes, and Henry, not knowing exactly what it meant, smiled, feeling forgiven. After Nanima passed away, Henry became the head chef and partner in a successful Indian restaurant that served uniquely East African Ismaili-style cooking such as samosas made with an extremely thin pastry, curries and stews in coconut, and some other dishes, that were a fusion of Gujarati and coastal African food.

Nanima also disliked my father and nicknamed him "Hashmo," a corruption of his real name, "Hasham." Yet she was forced to be nice to him, as it was the custom among Indians that sons-in-laws had to be pampered and flattered so they would not mistreat the daughters. Since my father had a terrible temper and often sent my mother into her grandmother's arms for comfort and advice, nanima would say in anger, "I should never have given your hand to that rascal."

My oldest aunt, Jena, was a laughing Buddha, moonfaced, with suspiciously black hair, oiled and parted in the middle and always wore a diamond-studded nose ring. She presided over her large family, four boys and five girls, firmly and good-naturedly, with a mischievous twinkle in her eyes. She had married a rich merchant and lived in a two-storied mansion, a Mediterranean villa with large French windows that opened onto a huge garden filled mostly with roses. On one side, she had a vegetable and fruit garden with pomegranates, a mango tree, and some plum trees. I looked forward to going there, walking in her garden, and stealing a plum or a peach. I loved hard, crunchy fruit fresh off the tree.

Aunt Jena's home was close to the Government House, where the present Imam, Karim Aga Khan and his brother Prince Amin were raised during the Second World War. The two brothers had been sent to Nairobi from Switzerland, to escape the war in Europe. She would recount years later in an indulgent tone that the two brothers would throw stones at the mangoes in her garden.

Jena masi called me *kario*—the dark one—but to soften the blow, she would add that I was *Shyam*, a term used to describe darkish Lord Krishna. She had an obsession with colour and even hired servants who were mullatos or coffee-coloured blacks. When she swore, she would say, "*Dedh na petno*", offspring of a street sweeper, the lowest caste. The caste system was part of her upbringing. It was a bit of a joke in the family that Jenabai, who liked fair skin, was married to Mohamedbhai, who was a rather dark man. To me, he appeared, with his curly hair and broad nose, to have a tinge of African blood.

My other two aunts, Gulbano and Malek, were earnest and read a great deal. Yoga, philosophy, and psychology would be mixed; baked and fed to anyone they could corner.

****

Nanima went to the mosque every Friday and would command the family to accompany her. After special *majlises* (prayer meetings) she would serve warnings to her granddaughters, saying, "You will die old maids if you continue to be picky and end up with some old worthless crow when nobody comes calling."

My cousins were choosy and turned down several good matches, though nanima tried hard to get them married into good families. The mosque was, and still is, a place for match making. After the service, some members of the congregation, usually the younger ones, met, flirted, or eyed each other around the dividing line. Nowadays, the mixing is much freer. Mothers sometimes introduced a young man and woman to each other, having agreed between them that the pair was suitably matched. Even now, a couple of our friends have introduced their suitable sons to Sameena, and she, like my cousins, has stubbornly ignored these introductions.

I remember many of the discussions that took place after one of my unmarried cousins had been introduced to a young man. Upon being questioned about her initial impressions, she replied that the man looked wimpy and boring and had a big nose and oily hair. Nanima responded that the party was well off, from a good family, ran a good business and would be a good provider. She would fling a dirty look at my quiet grandfather and add, "Look at what I've had to put up with!" She eventually retired to bed, shaking her head and mumbling to herself.

My grandfather was a reclusive, white-haired, and wrinkled old man by the time I knew him. He always had a crew cut. All he wanted was to be left alone with his pack of Clipper cigarettes. He loved Indian sweets, and every afternoon, he could be seen at the Indian Sweetmart, near Government Road, with his plate of *ladoos* and *pendas* or at a famous establishment called Ismailia, having samosas and extra sweet tea. I would occasionally bump into him and he would treat me to a snack. It would be a silent meal, he would sip his tea noisily and eat his ladoos with relish, oblivious to everyone around him.

Nanima and Nanabapa rarely communicated, though they shared a bedroom. Nanabapa would continue to smoke in bed. Sometimes, when we got up in the middle of the night, the tip would be visible, brightening as he drew in the smoke. The smoke bothered her.

My cousin Shiraz and I tried to help her with some attempts to reduce his smoking. He and I, along with his sister Hamida, spent many school vacations at nanima's place and often disturbed the peace. We started by stealing nana's cigarettes and surreptitiously smoked them in the backyard, justifying the theft as an altruistic action carried out to help nanima. Nana would run out of his cigarettes during the night and would wonder out loud why the count had suddenly decreased (we had not realized that he kept an exact count of the remaining cigarettes in his pack). Nanima would answer back: "*Saithe buddhee nathee*—at sixty, the brain leaves you."

As we grew older, we graduated to more serious misdemeanours and stole small amounts of Uncle Amir's whiskey. We were soon caught with liquor on our breath and given beatings by our horrified mothers. My Aunt Gulbano would say, with some justification, to my mother, "It is your son, Manu, who is the trouble maker."

****

Since nanabapa had no interest in being the head of the family, the role of patriarch fell to Rajab mama, my eldest uncle. He had fought for the British during their campaign against the Italians in Abyssinia (now Ethiopia), was wounded in the leg, and had returned sick with malaria. After recovering in a military hospital, he found himself demobilized and penniless. A friend suggested that he become a bookie since English horse racing was becoming a passion in Nairobi. Nanima gave him whatever she had saved and he set up shop as a turf accountant, the title by which the bookies were officially known.

By the time I was ten, I had learned a great deal about English horse racing. I knew when the famous meets like the Derby, the One Thousand and Two Thousand Guineas, were being held and how to place a bet. The names of jockeys like Lester Piggott, were frequently and enthusiastically discussed at Nanima's dinner table, and family members, including my aunts, often made money from a furtive bet or two.

I would often end up at the betting shop on evenings when big races were being run. If money had been made, Amir mama, my younger uncle, would slip me a ten- or twenty-shilling note. He also looked after my financial needs, such as school fees, when my father was going through a losing streak. Occasionally, he took me to films like *Mirza Ghalib,* starring his favourite actress and singer, Suraiya. It was through him that I got interested in the poet Ghalib. Even though I didn't understand most of the poetry, the majesty and sadness touched me. Over the years I continue to read translations of Ghalib, one of the great Indian poets of modern times. Apart from being the court poet of Bahadur Shah Zaffer, the last Mogul, who was exiled by the British for his part in the Indian "Mutiny" of 1857, Ghalib was also a philosopher and nationalist who tried to get the Hindus and Muslims to unite in the struggle against the British.

And when I grew up, Rajab mama let me read or browse through his large eclectic collection, including books as disparate as works about Sigmund Freud and history of the campaigns of Genghis Khan.

Once he made his fortune as a bookie, Nanima insisted that it be shared with his brothers. As Kenyan independence drew closer, however, he decided that it would be better to sell his assets and move to England. Infighting then broke out among the brothers over the sharing of the proceeds. He was not left with much. He tried his hand at a number of new businesses that failed, and late in life was reduced to living in a Council house in London. But his clear focus on his children's education has paid off. One of them, Moez, became an engineer and started building mobile networks in Africa, a business that has made him a fortune. Like his father, he is an understated man who still helps out family members who need looking after.

After Nanima's death, other members of the family would go to visit my Sultan mama on Sundays with dishes cooked by Henry. Following independence, whatever remained of institutions left by the British had sunk into disrepair and neglect. One day, a phone call brought tragic news. Sultan mama had disappeared. Apparently, he had jumped over the fence and disappeared into the village of Mathare, a huge and dangerous slum that had exploded into existence as Nairobi had expanded. Some investigations were made, and the family believed that Sultan mama, in his sixties, had been murdered.

17. Progress at School.

Zahra was a spirited girl of thirteen, rather small for her age, who had her hand up for every question in Najma's class. She had insatiable curiosity, a sharp mind and was far ahead of the class in her understanding of what was being taught. In fact, she seemed to be one of the few children who read books at home.

She often joined Najma in the morning as we climbed the stairs to the classrooms.

"Hello, Miss, how are you today?"

"Good, thanks."
"Did you go out yesterday evening?"
"Yes, to a play."
"Oh, where did you see it? What was it about?"

She had my habit of asking multiple questions in one go, posing the problem for the listener as to which to answer first.

They continued their chat as they climbed up to Najma's floor and I dropped off at the second floor.

Najma had become something of a hit at the school. She taught English well enough for the principal to suggest that some of the teachers should sit in on her classes. Najma found that the kids were good at art, music, and poetry and was enjoying teaching them.

Many came to chat with her during recess and stopped to talk as we entered or left. Furthermore, I couldn't do anything without it getting back to Najma. Even going to the toilet was reportable.

At the end of one rather long day, I was standing at a urinal in the boys' washroom.

A gaggle of young boys stood behind me and asked, "What are you doing, Suh?"

I turned my head and glared at them, "What do you think?"

The flock fled, full of laughter, and surrounded Najma who was waiting outside.

In unison they sang, "Miss, Miss, Suh is doing soo soo."

By now, we'd acquired a few more identities. I was Uncle, Chacha (Urdu for Uncle), or Suh.

But Najma had more. She was Aunty, Chachi, Madum, or Miss.

****

After three weeks I was happy to see some progress being made by Farhad and Akhtar. They were both pleased to have the extra attention and didn't look at being separated from the class and needing special help as a mark of being backward. They considered it to be recognition.

Akhtar was reading faster and was generally more relaxed. His teacher told me the biggest change in him was an improvement in his confidence. He began answering a few questions in class. I insisted that when he spoke, he enunciate his words clearly. Sometimes I would sit a little farther away from him and make him speak loudly enough for me to hear him.

Once a week he wore a red and white uniform instead of his normal khaki and beige. He explained that it was for PT- physical training. I suspected this would be the only time in the week that he'd get any exercise. I asked who cleaned and pressed his uniforms so immaculately. He looked at me a little puzzled. I prodded again. "Do you do it? Do you give it to a *dhobi?* Or does your mummy do it?"

"Mummy, of course," he said, looking at me as if I had asked a strange question.

"Do you help her?"

"No. I do my homework, then sit and watch TV. Mummy cooks and cleans and Daddy works."

He seemed quite clear about prescribed gender roles.

Farhad was also beginning to respond to my questions much faster. He showed a preference for writing. He would often quickly shape a couple of simple paragraphs with me on the laptop, and when I read them back to him, he seemed delighted.

When I showed Najma his essay, she thought he probably had a learning disability. He could compose but not comprehend stories or lessons from books. Unfortunately, there was no testing for such disabilities in the Indian school system and Farhad would not get any remedial help.

I didn't have many opportunities to meet any parents but one day, while I was sitting out in the sun after recess, two women wearing long frocks with their heads covered by pachedis approached me. It had become quiet after the children had gone back into the classes, the day was warm, the sky was clear and I felt relaxed sitting on the steps at the school entrance

One of them approached me tentatively and asked, "Could you please tell us where the principal's office is?"

"Just behind me. Go inside and turn left. It's just a few steps inside."

They didn't budge.

"Can we ask you something, bhai sahib?" she continued addressing me as an elder brother.

"Certainly."

"Are you a teacher?"

"I am volunteering as a teacher."

"Are most of the teachers volunteers?"

"No, No. There are very few of us here. I was in Mumbai on business and I decided to volunteer for a few weeks," I replied.

" *Baharna cho?*"

"Yes, I am a visitor from Canada."

"Ismaili?"

"Yes."

They broke out into big smiles and gave me the Ismaili greeting, *"Ya Ali madad"*.

"Maula Ali Madad ".

"And are you from outside Mumbai?" I asked.

The woman who had stayed silent so far, answered, "From Jamalia, a small town in Gujarat."

"Her son," she said, pointing at the first lady, "has just got a scholarship to finish high school. I am his *masi*. His name is Alim, the brightest boy in the school. Since it only teaches up to standard seven, we are here to drop him off him for the rest of his schooling."

"That sounds wonderful. Mumbai is a big place, where will he stay?"

"We have another sister and she has agreed to put him up. If our own blood won't help, who will?"

"Of course," I replied.

"Tell me, is it a good school? Alim is the first one to study so much. We want to be sure."

"I think it is a good school. But education has to be done at home too. Like homework, reading good books."

"Alim has his head buried in books all the time. He works very hard."

"Well, then, there should be no problems. He'll be fine."

"Thank you very much, bhai sahib. May Maula give you many blessings for this *seva,*" the masi said.

"Amen," the other one echoed.

They waved goodbye and went inside.

****

With two days of volunteering left, I visited Fakr-ud-deen for the last time.

As soon as I entered the shop, he said, "Come in, come in. I was hoping to see you before you left. I have good news. Have a *ladoo.*"

I popped the small, sweet *ladoo* in my mouth and after a few moments asked, "What's the celebration?"

"Lubina has had a proposal," Fakr-ud-deen replied, beaming.

"Oh, wonderful. Who's the lucky man?"

"My cousin Saifu-ud-deen's son, Zuber. Very educated. An engineer, you know."

I remembered that unlike the Ismailis, marriage between cousins is common amongst the Bohras.

"You have cousins in Pakistan?" I asked Fakr-ud-deen.

"Yes. Like your family, my family is also from Gujarat. During the Partition my *kaka* decided to go to Karachi, and my father came to Mumbai. My *kaka* felt he would have a better future in Pakistan. I was young, just a child, but I remember the arguments between my father and his younger brother. I think maybe he regretted his decision after going to Pakistan but he's too proud to admit it."

Fakr-ud-deen shows me a picture of Lubina, a beauty with large eyes, short curly hair, and a mischievous smile.

I wondered what she thought of all this.

"Has Lubina met him?" I ask.

"Once, when they were teenagers, almost twelve years ago. He has her picture and she has his. Both are happy with the arrangement. Now we will go to Karachi. Normally the boy's side should come here, but with all this trouble between India and Pakistan, it'll be better for us to go there."

"They'll meet before the wedding?" I asked.

"*Ek Dum*—of course. We are quite modern, you know. They will go to the cinema or a hotel for dinner. Zuber's sister will accompany them; they are still strict in Pakistan. Here I would let them go to the cinema on their own."

"And when would the wedding be?"

"*Arrey . . . Jat mangni aur pat vya.* A quick engagement and the wedding within days. Zuber is thinking of immigrating to the U.K. and the parents want him to get married before he goes. We will have a *nikah* and a simple celebration after which Lubina will return to Mumbai and wait for him to sponsor her."

The Muslim *nikah,* unlike the long Hindu *vivah,* full of chants, fire, horses, elephants, bands, and dances, is a very simple ceremony. A contract between a bride and a bridegroom is read out in the presence of witnesses. One of the conditions in the contract is that the groom promises a *mahr,* an agreed-upon sum of money, to be given to the bride at the time of the marriage or in the event of a separation.

Fakr-ud-deen, unlike a Hindu father, did not have to face the problem of paying a small fortune as the dowry to the groom. The nightmare of an Indian father is to have a clutch of daughters.

The dowry was an issue that came up all the time during our stay in Mumbai.

It was Jose our waiter at the Y who first brought it to my attention. He came from Goa where his ancestors were converted to Christianity by the Portuguese colonizers. Soon after we got to know him he shared with me his concerns about getting his daughter married off, particularly his worries about providing a dowry, a tradition that has persisted amongst converted Christians. To make matters worse, the dowry for a groom had increased dramatically in the last few decades to the enormous sum of five lakhs, about $10,000 US. It was, quite simply, a sum out of reach for a waiter who makes around $150 a month.

"Why has the dowry gone up so much, Jose?"

"Sa'ab, who knows? It's what they call inflation, and the foreigners with daughters bring bags of cash. Everybody wants to show off their riches. We poor people get caught in the middle of this madness."

"Have you saved enough, Jose?"

"Sa'ab, I can barely make ends meet."

"What does your daughter do?"

"A nurse, Sa'ab. Very happy, gets a good salary."

"So things will work out."

"She has received a few proposals but has turned them down."

Jose raised his hands upwards in a very Hindu gesture and said, "*Upperwale ke hath me hai*—It is in the hands of the One above, Sa'ab. I will keep looking at the matrimonials."

The search for a partner often starts, at least in the big cities, in the matrimonial section of a newspaper every weekend.

Matrimonials are grouped by caste. The largest portion in previous Sunday's edition of the *Times of India* was for Brahmins, about 50 ads out of about 300.

> Alliance for Pune based Bengali Brahmin. Mechanical Engineer 5' 8". Non Alcoholic, non Smoker. Having car and flat. Father retd. central govt officer. Seeks qualified Brahmin girl.

The smallest section belonged to the Scheduled caste (called Untouchables in the old days)—with just one ad:

> Groom Matang 28 5' 8" Fair, MBA working in Mumbai bank seeks same caste.

But this is not to say that all Hindus subscribe wholly to the caste system. There was a very small section (two ads) for those who didn't care for caste:

> Match Punjabi boy, affluent family 31/ 5 ' 8" Manager. Caste no bar.

But in most cases, the matrimonial section exhibits, clearly and publicly, the centrality of caste and family in Indian society. Academic qualifications, profession, and fairness of skin appear routinely.

Though fairness is highly desirable, the white Western woman poses a problem. On the one hand, she is fair skinned and alluring, but on the other hand, she often eats meat, especially beef. She uses toilet paper and not water, to cleanse herself, considered a backward and unhygienic practice. Another big minus is that she has too many opinions of her own. It's a dilemma. I think the fairness wins, helped by the fact that the whites were rulers once, a memory that has not completely vanished. But generally speaking, she is not good material for marriage as far as the family is concerned.

When Westerners appear confounded by arranged marriages, I imagine that at the back of their minds is the question of how two strangers can suddenly find themselves in bed on the wedding night and yet surprisingly have higher odds of staying married than their Western counterparts?

The family with the help of a matchmaker and a jyotishi often plans a wedding. The astrologer picks an auspicious day, the matchmaker helps determine dowry to be offered by the bride's family, after several hints from the groom's side passed through the intermediary.

The young accept this tradition, I think, because in Indian society, your first loyalty is to your family. You are conditioned, as a child, to consider yourself part of the family unit and not to think of yourself as an individual in your own right. Therefore, a marriage arranged by the family is not such a difficult step to accept and has always happened in this way.

But some wiliness is involved, too, and Indian society has always had a card or two to play to try to make sure that the marriage would work well. For one thing, most Indian families kept the sexes strictly apart until marriage, choosing instead to marry off the young people early, as in the case of our grandparents. A fourteen-year-old girl and certainly a sixteen- year-old boy who have been kept apart without having had the opportunity of looking at alternatives, would be more likely to happily embrace the arrangement. The hormones would kick in to take care of the rest of the situation.

Urbanization is changing things, but rural India still tries to marry its youngsters off early.

Perhaps the main reason why arranged marriages tend to last longer is that the level of expectation is lower than in the case of non-arranged marriages. In the West, romance and love are prerequisites, perhaps driven by Hollywood. In the Indian marriage, the main expectation is that the man does not drink or beat the wife and better still, treats his wife well. If he is educated, makes a good living and is liberal, that is wonderful. But he is not expected to take care of the children, do household chores (that's for servants or the women), or be the perfect soul mate that Western women look for.

This is not to say that Indian youngsters do not dream of love. Bollywood movies and soaps are rife with scenes of romantic longing. Here's a typical one:

A modern girl, upon hearing of a proposal, tells her mother, "But I don't love him, Mummy."

The mother smiles wisely, strokes her baby's head gently, and says knowingly, "It will come later, you'll see. Look at dad and me. I felt the same way. Now I can't live without him."

"But I love my Kishore."

"Baby, think about it. Will your boyfriend's family accept you? They are *paisaawala* ; we are poor. How will we pay the dowry? "

The conversation continues with blandishments, blackmail, and family opposition.

The girl gives in and agrees. In fact, she finds perfection in the chosen one and falls in love with him.

Perhaps the most attractive feature of arranged marriages is that it takes away the difficulty of finding a partner. Large, plain, or whatever, there is a partner for you. No bars, no angst, no worrying about shelf life.

****

Back at the Fancy Goods Store across from the school, Fakr-ud-deen interrupted my train of thoughts and said, "Mehboob-bhai, I want to ask for some advice from you."

"Sure, if I can help."

"Zuber is thinking of going to either the U.K or Canada. America is very hard to get into from Pakistan. You immigrated to Canada. What are your thoughts on where to go?"

I replied carefully: "Immigration is always a difficult and lonely experience in the beginning. It took Najma and I years to settle down and feel comfortable, but the reward was great. I prefer Canada because I think the Canadians are more welcoming than the British, but these days, that's maybe not so. There are many Indians in England that are well settled. I would say go where there are the best opportunities for their line of work and where there are the most number of friends and family."

"That sounds like good advice."

"Now tell me," Fakr-ud-deen goes on, "you told me you may have relatives in Pakistan. Are you planning to visit them?"

"I want to, but I hear so many things that make me very uncomfortable about Pakistan."

"Like what?"

"I hear about bad government, corruption and especially how they treat women there."

"Of course, there is bad government and corruption. But you know, a lot of newspaper-*wallahs* make things sound dangerous; it's good for selling their papers. And many politicians in India make Pakistan sound terrible and Pakistani politicians do the same against India—it gets votes. For the women, yes, there are problems. Najma bai will have to dress modestly, which she does. Better not to wear jeans and to cover the head. But there are many things that make it worth going—you will be surprised how beautiful parts of the country are, and what a language the Pakistanis speak! *Urdu- masha-allah*—language of *firashtas*. I always think that angels must speak Urdu. Mind you, I would never advise anyone to settle there but a visit, for someone like you who has travelled around the world, no problem!"

"Your advice is sound, Inshallah, I shall go to Pakistan to seek out my father's family."

****

There are two stories in particular that I didn't share with Fakr-ud-deen but which have left deep impressions on me and come to mind as soon as Pakistan is mentioned.

A close friend of mine, Shiraz, who is an expert on land management and digital mapping related this account of a meeting with a senior Pakistani government official who had asked to meet him.

He put up a map from a satellite and started his presentation by saying, "This line that divides the brown from the green areas is the border of Pakistan and India. The green side is India, the result of their green revolution, and the brown side is Pakistan."

Shiraz knew that the aides accompanying the senior official would not welcome comparisons with India, especially those that showed them in a poor light.

The senior official asked, " Are you saying that India is doing a better job than Pakistan?"

" I'm afraid so."

The room went quiet.

" Just tell me the truth."

Shiraz then told them that the land issues he had been asked to look into were not technical, about water management, irrigation, and farming techniques, but much more about empowering the small farmers and educating their children. He didn't spell out how they could do it because they knew the challenge. He has the gift of delivering hard truths with a very soft touch.

Later, he told me something of what he discovered about Pakistan. Land, he said, is still in the hands of the big landowners, who often demand that the tenants hand over half of what they produce, and refuse to invest in improvements. In the remote areas, landowners run entire towns and have private prisons, and most local people are enslaved through debt and usurious interest rates.

The most powerful force in Pakistan is the army, and the country has been run more by the generals, who routinely carry out coups, than elected officials. The army runs a large part of the economy.

The landowners have also moved into politics and created a coalition to oppose any attempts to carry out land reform. One landowning clan, the Bhutto family, has tried to modernize society and reduce the army's stranglehold. Zulfiqar Bhutto was hanged by the army; his daughter Benazir assassinated by persons unknown.

An extremely high rate of poverty and illiteracy has given rise to Islamic fundamentalism, which plays into the hands of *mullahs*. And the mullahs also control the country, along with the landlords and the army; not unlike feudal times in Europe when the church, the knights and their armies ran the country.

India, in every respect, has done the opposite. Nehru carried out land reform very early on after independence and removed the power of the large landowners. And the country has remained secular. It's lumbering democracy functions fairly legitimately, and the army has never ruled the country. Every attempt has been made to provide education, and the results are obvious.

Shiraz has never been invited back, not that he is keen to do so. And his wife doesn't want to go back either. She hates walking alone and is very uncomfortable in the markets dealing with men on her own and advises Najma not to go.

The second story is that of Zubeda, whom I met at a music party in Toronto.

The music party is a peculiarly Indian affair where one sits on the floor in someone's home to listen to a recital of poetry and/or music. During a break, I went out for some fresh air and noticed a woman strolling in the garden. She was a striking looking, somehow a larger than life figure who looked sad and forlorn.

A friend standing next to me told me her story.

During the previous year her husband had taken their Canadian-born daughter, Yasmin, to Karachi to meet with his family. The father, an artist, rented a home for a few weeks. They gave a party given in her honour, where a young man met her and was completely taken up with her.

In a few days, a proposal was sent for her hand. It was politely declined and the suitor was told that Yasmin was not interested. The young man persisted, phoned her up, and asked to see her. A few days later, Yasmin's boyfriend from Toronto, a young Ismaili called Alnoor, arrived to stay with Yasmin and the father.

After a week, the young man phoned up the father and said it was most un-Islamic to leave his daughter alone with a young man while he went out of the house.

The father politely told the suitor to mind his own business

The suitor came by a few days later with a *mullah*, who lectured the father about the inappropriateness of an outsider, a young man and not even a true Muslim, living in the house alongside his unmarried daughter. It would be wise to bring an older companion into the house, he advised.

The father, furious at the pair, asked them to leave.

The young man returned the next day.

Both Yasmin and her father were working downstairs while Alnoor was in the bathroom upstairs.

The spurned man shot both father and daughter dead.

Alnoor was wounded when he came down to investigate the shots. The assailant fled.

We came to know Zubeda a little in the following months, mainly because she shared Najma's interest in abstract art. Four years after the senseless and tragic killings, she had decided to sell all her belongings and return to Pakistan.

We happened to meet her the day before she was set to leave.

Her final words were, "I have my brothers and sisters in Karachi and there is nothing but memories of my husband and daughter here. Where else can I go? It's a terrible mess but Pakistan is still home."

****

Fakr-ud-deen continued with his own reservations about Pakistan.

"Between us, I only agreed to let Lubina marry Zuber after he told me he was going to emigrate. I didn't want my daughter to settle in Pakistan. Anyone with a good education gets out of there. The army and the politician *goondas* won't let go, there's no future in that country," he said.

As I prepared to leave Fakr-ud-deen got up, took my hand in both of his and with great affection said, "Mehboob bhai, please come to see me when you come back. I did not get the opportunity to entertain you and Najma behen this time, but my wife and I would like to take you out the next time."

"If Zuber and Lubina come to Toronto, tell them to come and see us. Najma can make a great *biriyani,* almost as good as the best Bohra biriyani," I replied.

Fakr-ud-deen smiled.

"Thank you. I have enjoyed your company, Mehboob bhai and learned a lot from you."

"And I from you, Fakr-ud-deen bhai."

18. Goodbyes.

The boys came in to say goodbye.

Farhad came in first, and I gave him the remaining books I'd bought for him. I'd been giving him one book a day for the last four days.

"Mine?"

"Yes."

"To take home?"

"Yours to take home and read. Read as often as you like."

"This is your last day?"

"Yes, I have to go back. My children need me in Canada."

"Will you come back soon?"

"I don't know, Farhad." I put my hand on his shoulders. His eyes were wet.

"But I hope to come back next year."

He continued to be silent.

"Maybe you can give me Sharik's number."

He perked up and gave me the number.

"He'll answer even if he's driving the taxi," he assured me.

We hugged, I let him go reluctantly, and he walked slowly out of the library. We both knew we might never meet each other again.

Then Akhtar came in with his teacher.

"These books are for you."

He carefully put them in his satchel.

"Will you read them?"

"Yes, and my Papa is going to buy me a computer like yours after the seventh class."
He did not like emotional displays.
We solemnly shook hands and he left.
I knew I would remember them both vividly, and I decided that if I ever went back to Mumbai, I would look them up.
I read through their journals.

My name is Farhad. My family has nine people, mummy, daddy, chacha, chachi, dada, dadi and mama, mami and my brother Sharik. Sharik is 21 and drives a taxi. He has a cell phone. He takes me to Sakinaka every Sunday to see my dada and dadi. She make the best Biriyani in the world. Biriyani is my favourite food. I also like films.

My favourite is Dhamal. My favourite scene is where police chase four goondas in a jeep. When I become twenty-one, I will become a policeman and buy my own Tata Sumo car. I will go to Sakinaka and take apples and bananas for my dada and dadi. And also buy my nanima a dupatta. She likes the green colour. I go to mehfil every day except Sunday. My daddy takes me there on a scooter. There Janabji teaches me Urdu for two hours, from six to eight.

I continue with Akhtar's journal.

My name is Akhtar. My family has five people Mummy, Daddy, Waqi, Dadi, and me. We live in one room. We have a TV. Waqi and I like watching Tom and Jerry. Daddy goes to masjid every Saturday and Sunday. I do my wazoo before prayer. I wash my hands, feet, mouth and face. Sometimes he takes me to an aquarium on his scooter. I like watching the blue and white fish.

Last week at Eid two friends came to play at home with me. They are called Haskin and Nabila.

Farhad clearly loved to write though I haven't included his attempts to write short stories here.
While I was packing up my computer, the boys came back with their classroom teachers and gave me their gifts, wonderfully drawn cards.

"Did Farhad and Akhtar draw these cards?"

"No, another boy and girl, the best artists in their class drew them. The boys have written their thank you's in their own hand, though."

The two young artists were also present, so I went over to shake their hands.

Najma told me that this was by far the best school in terms of encouraging art, and in terms of the level of interest the children had in art, that she'd seen in her twenty-year career as a teacher.

By contrast, the school system back home is always cutting courses like art and ESL (English as a Second Language) when there is the slightest budget upset. For a country increasingly made up of immigrants, this didn't' make sense to us.

Najma received a wonderful book on art from her classes, and we walked out of the school feeling extremely sad.

It was a horribly hot day, and I couldn't imagine teaching here in the monsoon season. The air felt sticky, and thick like a daal. I breathed heavily, probably a combination of the newly acquired weight and the pollution in Mumbai. I felt unfit. I'd put on ten pounds in India. After each major meal, there were offers of deserts: "Rasmalai, Gulab Jamans, Sa'ab?" I just couldn't refuse them.

****

After school, I dropped Najma off at Kala Niketan, the famous sari shop, and asked the driver to take me to the Crossword bookshop.

The middle-aged cabbie had a beaten down look about him. I felt compelled to find out why. I told him I was a writer investigating the lives of taxi drivers and looking for as much detail as I could.

Words started to flow like in a confessional. He spoke in a Hindi patois from the North.

"This is not my taxi, sahib. Like most cabbies I drive for the owner. On a daily basis."

"Daily basis?"

"I start at 7 and finish at 7, when I give the daily takings to the owner. If I don't make enough for a few days, he may give the cab to someone else."

"How much does he give you a month?"

"I am lucky if I clear 5,000 rupees a month. I spend 1,500 on myself and send 3,500 to the family."

"Where do they live?"

"In (Uttar Pradesh), Uncle, *goan mey*, in the village."

"How can you live on 1,500 rupees?"

"I share a room with six other cabbies and we pay four hundred rupees each. The rest is to fill my stomach."

"No women in your lives?" I tried to joke.

"If I could afford to keep another woman, I would, but I don't even have the energy. There are other more pressing problems."

I stayed quiet.

"Take yesterday. I drop off a fare near Nariman Point and start heading to Worli to drop off the cab. A rich-looking Madam hails me. She wants me to drop her off somewhere in Pedar Road, and it's going to make me late. Giving the car back late makes the owner angry. I tell her politely to find another car. She is angry and a *hawaldar* walks up to us. Policewallahs! He wastes half an hour, and though I beg him and plead with him and explain my circumstance, he gives me a ticket."

"What for?"

"You cannot refuse to take someone between 7 and 7. Now I have to go fight the case because the fine is a month's suspension. I'll have to bribe someone or there'll be nothing to send home."

"You can bribe them?"

He laughs mirthlessly. "Every month a third of my takings is given for bribes, stopping too long, U-turns, the list is endless."

"You must hate the police."

"They have to make a living too, Sa'ab."

"What about the government?"

"They don't want us here. They say you came here on your own. Go back to the village. But I can't make a living there."

I got off and gave him a hundred rupees. He searched around and gave me the change. I looked at him and returned the change.

His parting comment: "Put this in your writing, Sa'ab. Many days I want to end it and commit *khud kushi*.."

I don't think I'll forget the look on his face.

I didn't know what to do. I looked at him and reached out. "Take care of yourself, bhai."

I watched him drive away and turned to enter Moshe's inside the Crossword bookstore. One of the young waiters came up and said, "Lime and soda, sir?"

I nodded and sat down. The TV was showing footage of the handsome Salman Khan and the gorgeous Katrina Kaif, Bollywood stars, getting out of a limousine for some huge Bollywood wedding.

I sat quietly and wrote until Najma came in. We browsed through the bookstore and picked up a couple of books by Indian authors and a translation of Ghalib's poetry. As we left Crossword for the final time, I noticed that Priti and Pappu were not sitting in their usual spot in front of the store.

I located them around the corner from the shop. Every time I saw them I wanted to gather them up and put them in a tub full of warm water, boats, and ducks and let them play. I thought of Abid and Sameena frolicking in the ocean and splashing water at each other. Priti and Papu will likely never do that.

Whenever I'd gone into Crossword and they were there, I had to decide whether to ignore them, give them some money Did I have enough small denominations?, I thought) or should I bring them some food. It's too tough to agonize over the homeless in India; you couldn't maintain your sanity..

But somehow Priti and Pappu were different. I saw them every day, and they reminded me of Abid and Sameena as children.

I squatted down and said, *"Kaise ho?"*

How were they? A pointless question perhaps? Did they know?

They giggled as I handed over a hundred-rupee note. I had no smaller denominations

Priti took it and just held it. Where would she stash it? I wondered. Who would she give it to? Did she know it was a hundred? I would have given more if I felt she could manage to hold onto it.

Farhad and Akhtar had a chance of escaping poverty; Pappu and Priti, barring a miracle, none.

I ruffled their dirty manes, got up, and left them playing in the dirt, letting the fine dust slip through their fingers. They looked happy and I felt helpless.

I suppose no city could cope with such a massive influx of new immigrants. Most of Mumbai had become more like a huge camp than a city. Only parts of Mumbai,, perhaps two or three kilometres along the coast line, is what I think of as a city, with reasonable shops, restaurants, and theatres. Most of the rest seem like one massive overcrowded tenement. Pockets of slums blight the place.

****

That evening, though we'd been told not to give tips to the YMCA staff, we gave a few hundred rupees each to Jose and Chandu, who looked after us with such care and kindness. They made us part of their Indian family. We knew about the health problems of their relatives and difficulties in getting jobs and husbands for their girls. They knew what Abid and Sameena did and were happy for our good fortune. There were no pretences in our relationship. They talked about their problems freely and compared to theirs, our problems are insignificant. They simply assumed that all humans have the same challenges in life, health, jobs, bringing up children, and securing a good marriage and that there was no shame in sharing what one could with friends.

Both Jose and Chandu were close to retirement. I sensed they both believed in the Hindu notion of the four stages of life: the *brahmachari* (the student phase), the *grahasththa* (the married, childrearing stage), *vanaprastha* (the retired stage), and the *sanyansin* (the time for becoming an ascetic to seek the ultimate truth). Not much is mentioned about stages of a women's life except as supporting roles and always needing protection by men.

Both men make the same comments: "Sahib, I've done my duty, had a family, raised the children. I've done what God intended me to do. Whatever time is left is a bonus."

Their talk of death was very matter of fact. It was just the end of the last leg of this complex journey, not to be feared. Instead, it's a time to become respected for the wisdom acquired along the way.

We said goodbye to Jose and Chandu and flew out of Mumbai the next morning.

VII. 2009: RETURNING HOME

"Traveling—it gives you a home in a thousand strange places, then leaves you a stranger in your own land."

Journeys from 1325–1354 by Ibn Batuta

After a twenty-hour journey, jetlagged, I sat down in our living room, grateful to be safely back. The spotless room seemed larger and neater than I remembered and all that had been familiar, felt alien. We unpacked, opened the important mail, made a few phone calls, ate an omelette and went to bed.

The next morning we went shopping for groceries. Toronto felt eerily quiet, the sidewalks were almost empty, the streets too wide, and the SUV's monstrous. It was a drizzly day and the wind shook our car.

At the supermarket, there was no noise and the customers went about unsmiling, some intently looking at shopping lists. Everyone was courteous and kept their distance. All the goods were neatly stacked, over-packaged, and labeled with bar codes and prices that precluded any possibility of bargaining.

We bought some basic necessities: fruit, cheese, and meat. The smiling but bored checkout girl gave us a standard greeting and thanked us for shopping at Loblaws. The bill was shocking. A hundred and fifty dollars would have bought us thirty delightfully tasty meals with "organic" ingredients in Mumbai.

Existence felt unnaturally orderly. Rules were observed; there was ample room for everyone to move and even special access for the disabled. It felt wonderful to go out on the tree-lined walking trail behind our apartment. I noticed that the dogs on leashes, were well fed and obedient and often rewarded with pats, even hugs and kisses. The owners walked diligently along with bags to pick up the poop.

Suddenly, I missed the chaos of Mumbai: the beckoning touts and the stalls on the sidewalks, the hooting on the streets, the smells, the colourful saris, the beggars, the skulking dogs and even the occasional cow demanding space and respect.

It seemed crazy to feel disconsolate.

I thought of Priti and Pappu getting up in their slum and Akhtar and Farhad preparing to go to school. I thought of Fakr-ud-deen's shop and his family and hoped that Lubina was now happily married. To help get over this disequilibrium I continued to read the *Times of India* online. The elections were finally over, and I was delighted with the results. The fundamentalists had been shoved aside; the Congress Party had won, and with its majority it could make the necessary changes. They'd appointed a much younger set of ministers. The youngest was, in fact, twenty-eight, Agatha Samna, a minister for rural development.

I hope to go back to the subcontinent, particularly to Pakistan to try to find my father's family. All friends, contacts and news coming out of Pakistan paint a bleak picture, especially in terms of personal safety. Inshallah I shall continue to explore India simply because it's a place in constant flux, bursting with life and vitality; the unexpected is always present.

****

As I was finishing this memoir, we settled down in an apartment sandwiched between St. George campus of the university of Toronto with its many Gothic revival buildings, libraries, bars and cafes and Yorkville, full of designer boutiques, fashionable restaurants, and expensive hotels. Embarrassed at living so close to luxury, we felt comforted by the fact that our neighbourhood, the Annex, lies outside Yorkville.

We started to look for interesting coffee shops and cafes and discovered the Holt Café, in the middle of a high-end fashion shopping strip, a great spot for people watching and one that served a great variety of affordable sandwiches and delicious pastries.

One day I overheard a little exchange between two strangers at the café that I will always remember.

I was standing in the lineup at the sandwich counter while Najma was getting the coffee. Ahead of me stood a young woman who struck up a conversation with a young man carrying a large backpack.

"Where are you from?"

"Ireland", he replied.

"Really! I am from Dublin."

"This place reminds me of Bewley's", he said.

"You're right, I went there when I was at Trinity".

"I went to Trinity too. Small world isn't it!"

The conversation stopped when his turn for being served came up.

As his order was being prepared, he asked,

"Do you like living here?"

"Oh yes, it's -like coming to the future!"

I picked up a chicken sandwich and a salad, found a table and waited for Najma still thinking of the girl's perfect choice of words… like coming to the future.

Watching people at a table outside the café is like watching the world walk by.

I don't think sitting at the Norfolk in Nairobi deciding where to go, we could have ever have imagined that we would end up in a city of such incredible diversity. I still feel awed by watching mixed couples and friendships between people from diverse backgrounds.

When we arrived we were part of two percent of the population called 'visible minorities'. Now more than half the population is made up of visible minorities. For Najma and I, the city's quiet transformation from a provincial, predominantly European society to a vibrant multicultural one, is a miracle.

My visits back to Kenya and India have brought the change into an even sharper focus. In Kenya I am aware of being an Asian. Most people I know still belong to a well-off group who live in gated communities or heavily guarded homes. The vast majority of the population is black and poor.

In India I am aware of being a Muslim in a Hindu society where caste and religion defines one's place in society.

I do feel the loss of the language that was my heritage, especially as far as my children are concerned. Living in Toronto, however, where my race and religion don't define me or place restrictions on where I live, work or who my friends are, more than makes up for it.

It's a city filled with hope, reminiscent of the early days of independence in Nairobi, when constructing a new order and society appeared to be within reach. I can live with this promise.

The End

GLOSSARY

I start this glossary with an explanation of the hierarchy of the Indian family and the rest of the section is alphabetically ordered by the terms used.

Family hierarchy:
Each family member in the hierarchy of the extended family has a specific name.

The Indian child learns to recognize the many authority figures apart from the parents very early in life.

As an example, unlike in the western world the word grandfather can be used to define both the maternal and paternal grandfather. In the Indian context there is a separate word for these two relatives.

The following are terms to describe the relatives I have written about
1. Nani - maternal grandmother.
2. Nana - maternal grandfather
3. Dadi - maternal grandmother
4. Dada - paternal grandfather
5. Mama - maternal uncle
6. Mami - maternal uncle's wife
7. Chacha - father's younger brother
8. Chachi - chacha's wife
9. Masi - mother's sister
10. Masa - masi's husband
11. Beta - son
12. Beti - daughter

Other terms.

akni: a pilaf
azaan: call to prayer
Bahut Achaa- very good.
Banya- Local shopkeeper/moneylender
Buda- big
Behen –Sister
Buddhu- a fool
bhakt: worshipper
bhai: brother
bhajan: Hindu Hymn
biriyani: a rich spicy rice based meal with chicken, beef or vegetables etc
Chaiwallah-Tea Vendor.
Chaprassi- Peon
chevdo: snack made from rice flakes, chick peas, potato sticks, seed, nuts etc
Dalit. Among the lowest in the Indian caste system
dargah: tomb
Desi- local Indian
dekhawa - ostentation
dhandha: business
dhow- Arab boat powered by a triangular sail, using the monsoon winds.
duka(Swahili)- Shop
Dua: a prayer (in this context the prayer Ismaili Muslims recite)
dubbas: tins
dukawallah – a Hindi/Swahili word for shopkeeper
dungafassad - civil disturbance
firman- Advice from the Imam.
ganthias: large, tortilla-like chips served with fried green chilis and spicy, shredded carrots and cabbage
Ginans – Ismaili hymns
goonda: thug
gora: white man
gudha: ass
Gupti- secret follower
gurudwara: Sikh temple
gusul committee: volunteer burial committee
haraam: forbidden
Harijan Untouchable
Hath kharchi: pocket money
hudtal: strike
idli: cream of wheat pancake
jalebi: fried sweet pretzel

karz- Debt
jaati-caste
jamat – the community
Jamat bhai: the Jamat khanna custodian
Jamatkhana/ khanna – Ismaili mosque
jawan: young Indian soldier
jyotishi: a holy man who reads astrological charts and chooses the name
kamadia: the mukhi's assistant
kamadiani: usually the kamadia's wife but sometimes just a female head of congregation
kedgeree : dish of rice and lentils
kirpan: ceremonial sword or dagger worn by Sikhs
Kirtan – prayer with hymns- usually Punjabi
Khushali – a   religious celebration (Ismaili)
kurta: loose fitting long shirt; kurti for shorter version for women
locho: mess
mard-- A man
mazdoor-manual labourer.
masjid:mosque
mukhi – the head man at Ismaili mosque
mukhiani- usually the mukhi's wife but sometimes just a female head of congregation
mzungu – white person
nandi: food offering taken to mosque to be auctioned, proceeds usually used for communal works
nasibdar: fortunate one
Naseeb- Fate.
paan: betel nut leaf wrapped around betel nuts and condiments to be chewed over a long period
pachedis - head covering
paisa: money
pani puri: popular snack of fried puree and tamarind juice
patla: very low wooden seat
peti: an accordion on the floor
 Pir- a holy man or missionary.
pishi: (Swahili) Cook
purees: fried bread
Rationwallah- general store-owner
rotlas: millet flatbread, often eaten with garlic, chilis, and yogourt
Satryagrah: practice of nonviolence.
sadharan: ordinary
saggawallah: relative

shabash-bravo
shamba (Swahili)– A orchard or plantation
sherwani: long coat worn by a man
subh: propitious
Sukhi- happy
suti: a piece of the pot in a card game
Sutee- woman burned on husband's funeral pyre
Suva dana – a mixture of dill, sesame, and coriander seeds sprinkled with sugar-coated aniseed (an after-dinner digestif)
tasbi: rosary
tabla: drums
tanta – a quarrel or disturbance
taweez: a talisman from a holy man to protect a person from evil and disaster
visi: home cooked take away meal
Wanainchi (Swahili): Sons of the land
Ya Ali Madat- Ismaili greeting- May Ali help you ; usual reply is Maula Ali Madat- may he help you too
zenana: the women-only compartment on a train

Made in the USA
Lexington, KY
13 December 2017